PENGUIN BOOKS

The Investor's Handbook

ProShare was founded in 1992 by HM Treasury, the London Stock Exchange and a consortium of major companies as an independent, not-for-profit company limited by guarantee. It is now funded through charitable donations from over 180 sponsor companies and by grants from the London Stock Exchange, the Gatsby Charitable Foundation and the John Templeton Foundation. ProShare's work is primarily in three areas: Individual Investment, Youth Education and Employee Share Ownership.

The Investor's Handbook

ProShare's No-Nonsense
Guide to Sensible Investing

PENGUIN BOOKS

PENGUIN BOOKS

Published by the Penguin Group
Penguin Books Ltd, 27 Wrights Lane, London w8 5tz, England
Penguin Putnam Inc., 375 Hudson Street, New York, New York 10014, USA
Penguin Books Australia Ltd, Ringwood, Victoria, Australia
Penguin Books Canada Ltd, 10 Alcorn Avenue, Toronto, Ontario, Canada m4v 3b2
Penguin Books India (P) Ltd, 11 Community Centre, Panchsheel Park, New Delhi – 110 017, India
Penguin Books (NZ) Ltd, Private Bag 102902, NSMC, Auckland, New Zealand
Penguin Books (South Africa) (Pty) Ltd, 5 Watkins Street, Denver Ext 4, Johannesburg 2094, South Africa

Penguin Books Ltd, Registered Offices: Harmondsworth, Middlesex, England

First published 2001
1

Set in 9.5/14 pt Linotype Sabon
Typeset by Rowland Phototypesetting Ltd, Bury St Edmunds, Suffolk
Printed in England by Clays Ltd, St Ives plc

Contents

Contents

Introduction

The stock market can be baffling. It has its own language, its own way of judging and reacting to economic news and trends, its own fads and fashions for particular shares, industries and business personalities. All this gives it a mystique that intrigues as well as bewilders potential investors who would love to get involved in the stock market if only they understood more about it. If you are one of them, then ProShare's *Investor's Handbook* is for you.

You may be one of the millions of investors who became

shareholders for the first time by applying for shares in British Gas, British Telecom or other privatizations. Maybe you have received 'windfall' shares from your building society when it floated on the stock market or perhaps you bought shares in an Internet start-up company during the 'dot com' hype and now want to know more about how it all works. Even if you don't hold shares directly, the chances are that your financial future is closely linked to what happens on the stock market.

Unit trusts, for example, have long been popular with investors. If you have a personal or company pension scheme or a savings plan or an endowment policy with an insurance company you will, one way or another, have your investments tied up in the stock market. These are all collective forms of investment where professional managers decide which shares or other investments to buy or sell. But the private investor is still faced with a baffling array of choices.

So there is no substitute for having a good working knowledge of the stock market when it comes to seeing through the sales patter and deciding what kind of investments will be best for you.

The incentives to save for the future have never been stronger. Investment in the stock market is now a crucial element in an individual's long-term financial planning. But it is probably the least well understood.

The Investor's Handbook takes you through the maze step by step. It aims to answer all your questions – plus some you may not yet have thought of. It tells you what you need to know about the stock market and how to make the best of it. When you have read this book you will have the basic knowledge you need to set about investing in the stock market. You won't always get it right – no one does – not even the professionals. But if you apply your common sense and judgement and keep your personal objectives firmly in mind you are likely to succeed. You will find the stock market fascinating – developing a real interest in financial events will be a crucial element in your success.

We hope this book helps you to enjoy learning more about the stock market.

Happy investing.

Wealth warning

The information contained in this book is intended as a guide only and does not constitute investment advice. ProShare does not accept liability for any of the decisions taken as a result of using this guide. Remember that the value of shares and the income from them can go down as well as up.

1

What are Shares and
Why Invest in Them?

What is a share?

A share in a company is just that. Buying shares in High Tech
Enterprises plc (HTE plc) makes you a part owner for as long
as you have them. Originally, our imaginary company would
have been privately owned, probably by the entrepreneur
who started the business. In order to raise capital for expansion, HTE plc shares are offered to investors through the
London Stock Exchange, essentially a market, where they
can be bought and sold at a price that reflects supply and
demand.

Why buy them?

Whether you buy them through a new share issue where a
company floats for the first time, have received them from
your building society or acquire them in the 'second-hand' (or
secondary) market which is the main business of the stock
market, the reasons for investing in the shares are the same.
You believe HTE plc is a company that is going to prosper
in the future. Its profits are going to grow over the years.
The dividend payments it makes to shareholders out of its
profits each year are going to rise so you look forward to an
increasing income.

You also expect the share price to rise – reflecting the profits and dividend growth which should make the company, of which you are a part owner, more valuable.

Buying shares is the most direct way of investing in the long-term success of a business – or indeed of the economy.

Shares are 'risk capital'

Companies can raise money in a number of ways. They can go to the bank and ask for a loan. The bank will retain some of the company's assets as security, receive interest on the loan and expect it to be repaid at the end of the agreed period. The bank does not get any direct benefit from the growth of the business. If profits fall, it does not affect its return. If the company fails, the bank, along with other creditors, has a claim on the assets. However, shareholders are last in the queue. They will receive some payment only if the company has assets left after all other creditors have been paid.

Shareholders' returns are not guaranteed.* Company profits can fluctuate – so can the dividend out of which they are paid. Most companies will try to maintain their dividend payments even in a recession. But a large fall in profits will usually mean a reduced dividend and a lower return for shareholders.

*There is always a risk that you won't get back all you invested – that's why it's referred to as 'risk capital'.

Share prices fluctuate as well – often in a way that baffles shareholders. There are almost as many theories as to why shares go up and down as there are shares – but here are some of the reasons:

- Good or bad news from the company

- The expectation of good or bad news from the company

- Take-over rumours

- Change of management

- Economic news and other external influences

We will discuss the impact of these and other factors in more detail in later chapters, as well as the effect of economic trends on share prices. Anticipating share price and market movements is one of the key elements of successful stock market investment. So getting your timing right is very important.

Why shares are different

While there are risks with shares, the potential for reward can be higher than other forms of investment. As an example, let us take the standard building society investment – one of the most popular ways to save money. You receive interest on your savings and the money is safe and easily accessible. Bank and building society savings are and should be an important part of your financial planning – but not all of it.

What is happening to the value of your capital?

When interest rates are high, as they were in the early 1990s, the return on bank and building society deposits may keep pace with inflation – or perhaps even better it. But when interest rates are relatively low, as they tend to be these days, you run the risk of the real value of your savings being eroded. There is a chance that your original capital will not grow to keep abreast of inflation. While you can receive a good income from shares (we will discuss this later), one of their main attractions is that the value of your capital should not be eroded because of inflation, which can happen if you leave your savings in a bank or building society account. As the chart on page 9 shows, over the long term, investment in the stock market has proved one of the best ways of maintaining the real value of your capital – and of increasing it. This is why it has a crucial part to play in your financial planning.

There are of course different kinds of strategies involved in stock market investment – and how you approach it depends on:

- the amount you want to invest;

- the time you are prepared to devote to it.

You should start off by investing in 'blue chip' companies – substantial corporations which are often household names, where a steady growth in dividends is the order of the day. You might want to find exciting 'high growth' companies, pin-point good recovery prospects, or speculate in 'penny' shares, but this should happen only when you have built up a sound portfolio of stable companies.

We will deal with all these in later chapters and so help you decide what kind of share portfolio you should have. But first, you have to look at your own financial position and decide how much of your money you should invest in the stock market.

What are Shares and Why Invest in Them?

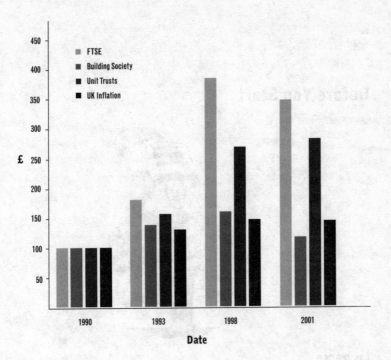

Value of £100 in January of each year shown

2

Before You Start

Insurance

If you have a job, a mortgage and a family, the most basic
first step in financial planning is to make sure you have
adequate insurance. That means life assurance, mortgage insurance – maybe permanent health insurance as well. What
would happen to your family if you died, or were unable to
work?

Pension

If you are in a company pension scheme, you may wish to
check your entitlements. If you have moved jobs several
times, your prospective pension may not look too wonderful.
Take advantage of the full tax relief available to top up your

pension – either by paying more into the company scheme by way of additional voluntary contributions (AVCs), or by investing in one of the many individual AVC schemes available from insurance companies. If you do not have a company pension or if you are self-employed, you should put some money into a personal pension plan.

Short-term cash fund

You should build up a fund of spare cash – money that you can put aside to earn a good return, perhaps in a bank or building society – somewhere you can gain immediate access in a crisis.

What are you investing for?

No one should have all their capital invested in shares – particularly if you are saving for specific items, such as school fees, where you are committed to spending at a certain point. Needless to say, buying shares is not the most appropriate way to save for a holiday, a deposit on a house, or a new car. What if your shares have fallen in value when you need the cash? A share portfolio should be a long-term investment. If you rely on your investments to produce a sizeable proportion of your income, you will need a high and predictable return from part of your portfolio – from gilts (government stocks), or guaranteed-income bonds for instance – or from shares that pay a higher dividend.

Long-term goals

Once you have decided on your immediate financial priorities, you can think about buying shares. The essence of share investment is to enable your capital to grow over the years.

For some people, their biggest concern is having enough money to retire on comfortably – maybe retire early (this may not be voluntary these days), change careers, or just go fishing. Others want to leave a nest egg for their children. To do all of these, you need to make your money work for you.

In the next chapter, we will take a closer look at the kind of shares you should be investing in and learn more about the workings of the stock market.

3

Types of Shares, Useful Jargon
and Measuring Performance

There are over 2,750 companies with shares quoted on the
London Stock Exchange. Some are billion-pound conglom-
erates, others are valued at just a few million pounds. They
represent the whole range of economic activity. Look at the
daily list of share prices in the financial press. There you
will find them divided into different sectors – motors, food
retailers, chemicals, oils, property, and so on. But how do you
set about choosing which areas are for you?

Spreading the risk

One fundamental rule of investment is to spread your risks –
don't put all your eggs in one basket. That means building

a balanced portfolio with holdings
in several different companies and
industries. If one sector or company
has a particularly bad time, you'll
have your other shares to see you
through. This doesn't mean, however, you have to stick only to big
safe companies (they can have bad
times too). There should be some
room for a bit of exciting speculation

in your portfolio – it's fun and that's where you can make some real gains – or suffer some losses! But it's important to balance your wilder hunches with solid shares. You should work out what proportion of your money you should invest where. *A sensible guideline would be 25 per cent of your portfolio in blue chip companies, 50 per cent in mid-cap companies (the FTSE 250) and 25 per cent in small-cap companies.*

Knowing your shares

Unfortunately shares do not come ready labelled 'low risk', 'high risk', 'sure-fire winner', or 'good old dependable'. But the stock market recognizes different kinds of shares – not just by size or industrial activity – as having particular characteristics. To build your portfolio you should get to know them.

Blue Chip companies

These are big established companies – such as Tesco, Unilever, ICI, BT and Shell. They are the 'first division' in financial terms with solid track records of substantial profits and dividends. They are large, valued by the stock market at over £5 billion – and form the backbone of the giant port-folios run by pension funds and insurance companies that need to invest in large quantities of shares. A lot is known about these companies – teams of stockbrokers' analysts spend their days researching them and producing regular reports. As a result, their share prices tend to be more stable than smaller companies, although there can be exceptions and the recent fall from grace of Marks & Spencer is a notable one. Due to their size, they normally reflect the general movement of the economy, the stock market and of their particular sectors. They are a sensible foundation for any portfolio.

Growth companies

Spotting one of these in its infancy – before it is generally recognized as something special – is every investor's dream. Typically, a growth company will be in an expanding sector of the economy where a go-ahead management has produced higher-than-average profits growth for several years in a row. It may have a unique product or a technical edge. For instance, anyone who bought shares in the pharmaceuticals company Glaxo Wellcome as a new issue, or in its earlier years, will have seen a handsome return.

The Internet has produced a new type of growth company with Internet or 'new technology' stocks. These companies typically have very little track record and will probably have made minimal, if any, profits. See Chapter 13 for more information about these companies.

These growth companies command a stock market premium – the dividend yield is lower and the price/earnings ratio is higher (see pp. 20–23) because investors are buying the prospect of faster-growing profits and dividends for the foreseeable future. But this 'glamour rating' is vulnerable if growth slows, as it invariably does. Investors need to be alert.

Recovery shares

Most companies reflect the general trend of the economy – but some shares really magnify the ups and downs. When times are tough, profits fall by more than average – but when things get better they can improve enormously. There can be good profits to be made from these shares if you get the timing right. Industries like house building, car components, electronics and furniture retailing are where you will find plenty of recovery candidates, particularly when the economy is coming out of recession – but check that the company is basically sound, with a previously good track record in terms of increasing turnover and profits. Details of how to do this are contained in Chapter 6. Individual companies that have fallen on hard times for one reason or another can be good recovery prospects too – look out for a change in management, for instance, which is likely to be reported in newspapers or on investment websites.

High-income shares

Many consider high-income shares less risky than the glamorous growth shares, because when the opportunities for profits growth may be poor, a good dividend yield means investors still get a decent return. High-income shares can give a good capital performance when the stock market rises as well, but you should choose carefully. A high yield can also be a distress signal – particularly one that is nearing double figures. It could well mean the shares are anticipating falling profits and a reduced dividend instead. You could be looking at a recovery share – or a company heading for the corporate graveyard.

Penny shares

These can be fun, offering you more shares for your money, which makes you feel good. But be warned – they are a gamble. They are priced at a penny because that is what the market thinks they are worth.

A penny share only has to move by a few pence to produce a very large percentage rise – that's the great attraction – or fall, and that's the great risk. One drawback is that penny share 'spreads', the difference between the current buying and selling prices, can be disproportionately large. Some penny shares are in companies where profits have fallen and might recover. Others may be 'shells' where the business is stagnant. They are a target for entrepreneurs who see them as a back door way of getting a stock market quotation for their own business. Anything can happen, and frequently does.

AIM (Alternative Investment Market)

AIM shares have proved very popular with private investors since the Stock Exchange created this entrepreneurial market back in 1995. It now has 400 companies quoted on it. The idea is to give new companies the chance to raise money without having to show a track record and conform to all the stringent regulations of the main stock market. In a very real way the creation of the AIM fulfils one of the main historical functions of the stock market – raising capital for new business ventures.

It is important to recognize that many of these companies are speculative, but the AIM includes exciting companies developing new processes and techniques in technology, biotechnology, health and other research-orientated fields as well as conventional businesses. But investors must be wary of some of the grandiose prospects held out by these companies and be prepared to do some serious research of their own. The ranks of the AIM include some big winners and some big losers.

Other markets

There are a number of other markets and exchanges open to private investors. Inevitably, some of these opportunities come with a risk warning, but for the more experienced investor, prepared to use the increasing amount of information available to research investments, there are companies being quoted on these markets and exchanges that have the potential to enhance a well-balanced portfolio.

- Techmark is the London Stock Exchange's share market within a market which brings together companies of all shapes and sizes, from a variety of sectors. These companies all have a commitment to innovation in common. This market makes it easier to invest in companies with a technology focus as they are all listed in one place. Go to www.londonstockexchange.co.uk for more details.

- Ofex was launched in 1995 to enable unquoted companies to offer shares in their companies to the public. Ofex generally draws companies that wish to raise smaller amounts of capital, predominantly from private investors. Many companies listed on Ofex go on to AIM and a handful have gone on to full listings on the main market.

- Nasdaq is best known as a market for high-tech shares and includes many household names such as Volvo and Fuji. Since 1971 it has grown to become one of the largest stock markets in the world, with over 5,000 companies quoted on it. Although it is based in the US, information on Nasdaq is quoted in the *Financial Times* and is available at www.nasdaq.co.uk.

- Since its launch in 1996 Easdaq has provided a market for European growth companies. UK investors can gain access to high-growth companies both UK and Europe-wide. Further information is available at www.easdaq.com.

When investing in foreign companies, things to bear in mind include the tax position and the costs of buying shares. Also be aware that exchange rates will have an impact on the performance of your investments. Some stockbrokers charge considerably more for transacting overseas trades, due to the complexity of settlement. You are sometimes better off finding a broker who has offices in the country in which you are trying to buy shares. Other brokers will insist that you have a minimum order size before they will trade for you. Further guidance on investing overseas is available in the ProShare Investor Update 16, 'Investing in Overseas Markets',* which is available from the ProShare website at www.proshare.org.

Useful share jargon

Some shares are described as defensive. This has nothing to do with jet fighters or tanks. It means that certain industries are less affected by downswings in the economy. Major food retailing companies for instance may be considered defensive – we all have to eat even in a recession.

Cyclical shares are the reverse of defensive. These are companies whose business and profits are very sensitive to economic trends – see 'recovery shares' (p. 15).

'Highly geared' sounds painful and can be. Highly geared

*See **Chapter 16**, pp. 138–40, for a complete list of Investor Updates and details of how to obtain them.

companies have large borrowings by comparison with their share capital. When interest rates rise, the increased cost of those borrowings can make a big dent in profits, magnifying the effect of any slowdown in the company's actual trading results.

The term 'highly rated' can apply to a whole share sector where future prospects are considered to be particularly good – or to an individual company. The stock market puts a high value on these companies compared with the average.

Monitoring your shares

Why not pick some individual shares for a hypothetical portfolio? Keep track of them for a few weeks. Watch how they respond to economic news, company news and the general trend of the stock market.

Later in this book we will take a detailed look at analysing individual companies. But you can't start to look at shares without understanding the two main yardsticks by which the stock market evaluates them – the dividend yield, and the price/earnings ratio.

Dividend yield

A dividend is the amount of income paid each year per share to investors. The 'dividend yield' is the return from the income, expressed as a percentage of the money you paid for the share. In practice it is complicated to work out. Dividends are paid by companies with a 10 per cent tax credit already deducted but the yield is worked out on the gross amount – before tax is taken off. We will deal with the personal tax aspects of owning shares later. For the moment you can look at the share listings in the financial press. Most show the dividend yield of each share listed. What are those yields telling us?

- A very high yield may be a sign that the company is expected to cut its dividend. The share price has already fallen in anticipation of reduced profits – but the yield is reflecting last year's pay out and not the lower amount expected.

- A low yield often indicates that a company's profits, and therefore dividends, are expected to grow faster than average. The share price has risen in anticipation of this rising income.

- Relative yields are a useful way of comparing shares. A company whose shares are yielding lower than the sector average may grow faster than one that is yielding higher than average.

Yields on shares are the stock market equivalent of the rate of interest paid by other kinds of investments. Because the stock market offers the prospect of capital growth as well as an annual return, average dividend yields are lower than, say, the return from a building society, where the amount of the capital goes neither up nor down.

Price/earnings ratio

The price/earnings ratio is the stock market's other main tool for comparing one share with another. It tells you how many years it would take for the net profits after tax (known as earnings) to equal the current share price. We will explain earnings in more detail later (pp. 63–6).

Assuming a company makes 10p a share earnings, and the

share price is 100p, then the price/earnings ratio is 10 (100p divided by 10p of earnings).

The price/earnings ratio is often simply called the 'p/e' ratio. Sometimes people use the expression 'so many times earnings', or 'so many years' earnings'. They all mean the same thing.

Many newspapers publish price/earnings ratios in their share price lists. Once again, they can be misleading because they are calculated on last year's historic profits. Like dividends, they tell us different things.

- A high price/earnings ratio generally means that the company is expected to grow quickly, and increase earnings rapidly, but might also be an indication that the share at its current price is overvalued.

- A low price/earnings ratio effectively indicates that the company is rated a plodder, or one whose profits might fall, or it could be undervalued.

- Like relative yields, relative p/e ratios are a useful way of comparing shares. A company whose shares have a lower p/e ratio than the sector average may grow faster than one that has a p/e that is higher than average.

You might hear the stock market pros talking about a 'prospective' or a 'forecast' p/e ratio. This means that the calculation has been made on the basis of earnings that the company is expected to produce in the current year or in the future.

Unlike dividend yields, price/earnings ratios cannot be compared with returns on other forms of investment.

4

Buying and Selling Shares

Many investors had their first taste of the stock market through a privatization or a new issue – the sale of shares in a company 'floating' on the market. You fill in the application form, send off the cheque and, if you are lucky, get the shares you want. Many other investors have received shares for the first time through the demutualization of their building societies. Easy. But then what?

When it comes to buying more shares – or selling the ones you've got – many new investors are uncertain what to do next. You may want to trust your own judgement from the start. You may want to take advice. Or you may want to find someone who will manage your financial affairs for you. Don't be put off by fears that no one is interested in the small investor. An increasing number of firms are, particularly with the advent of on-line stockbroking, but to get the kind of service you want, you will have to do a bit of research.

Where do you go next?

To buy and sell shares you need to use the services of a stock-broker. Today, many high street banks and building societies provide stockbroking services. It is important to understand that one stockbroker can be very different from another in the services they offer. A stockbroking firm may be part of a huge financial conglomerate in the City, or it may be an independent company specializing in private clients.

There are many good stockbrokers outside the City – and other firms who are mainly interested in institutional business from large investors. Before you approach a stockbroker, you should find out what kind of firm it is. A free directory of private client stockbrokers, *The Association of Private Client Investment Managers and Stockbrokers (APCIMS) Directory)*, gives details of firms and the services they offer, which makes choosing a suitable stockbroker much easier for you.*

Banks have been keen to advertise their services to small shareholders in recent years – you can now go into some

---

*See **Chapter 16, Useful Addresses,** for their address and how to obtain this directory pp. 141–2.

branches and buy shares at the touch of a button. Many banks own stockbroking companies – even if yours does not, it should be able to buy and sell shares through a stockbroker on your behalf.

Some building societies offer share-dealing services. If you were lucky enough to have received windfall shares you should have been sent information on share ownership.

Many banks, building societies and larger stockbrokers now have on-line broking services and there are numerous other on-line broking services keen to attract private investors, so shop around and speak to a number of brokers about their services and charges before you make a decision.

You can buy and sell shares through independent financial advisers (IFAs) too. They will not be members of the London Stock Exchange but they will place your orders with a London Stock Exchange member firm.

What kind of service do you need?

The APCIMS Directory explains the range of services available from each stockbroker. But before you choose a firm you have to decide what kind of service you want.

Dealing or execution only

This is the most no-frills dealing share service for those who don't need advice or help with financial planning. Many stockbrokers offer this kind of low-cost service – taking orders by telephone or post and increasingly on the Internet where investors can transact orders electronically from their personal computers.

Most banks, some building societies and the specialist telephone services offer an execution-only service. If you are very confident of your own judgement – or only want to buy and sell shares very occasionally – an execution-only service could be the cheapest option.

However, it should be stressed that no personal advice is given – and investors are on their own when it comes to decision making. None the less, execution-only brokers have developed a wide range of services for investors that include useful information on both individual shares and the stock market in general in the form of newsletters or information websites. Recently, there has been a proliferation of investment-related websites providing information for private investors. More active investors may find it worthwhile to select a service which charges a joining fee or annual charge but where the minimum commissions on each deal are low. So if an execution-only stockbroker sounds right for you, there is a whole variety of different services on offer depending on how active an investor you want to be.

Advisory

If you want someone to talk to and advise you on stock market investment you will find that some stockbrokers offer an advisory service (dealing with advice) for investors who want to take the final decisions themselves. If you want to take an active interest in share investment without going it alone this more traditional stockbroking service might appeal to you. You may pay a little more (for instance, minimum commissions per deal may be higher) but it normally gives you access to the firm's own research and investment analysis – and you get a sounding board for your own ideas. The stockbroker may also call you with investment suggestions.

An advisory service is 'non-discretionary' meaning that the

final decisions on what shares to buy are always left up to you and nothing will be bought or sold without your say so.

There are different kinds of advisory services, ranging from purely reactive services where a stockbroker only responds to your requests for advice on specific shares, to more proactive services where your stockbroker keeps tabs on your whole portfolio as well as providing other services, such as regular valuations. Some stockbrokers stipulate a minimum size of investment before they take on a client. Others may want to establish how active an investor you are likely to be.

There are plenty of stockbrokers specializing in individual investors. You may get a recommendation from a friend who is already a client. Finding the right stockbroker is as important as comparing costs.

When it comes to choosing an advisory stockbroker there is absolutely no substitute for meeting the person who will be dealing with your account face to face and making sure that you both know what your personal investment objectives are. It is important that you feel comfortable talking to the person who will be your main contact.

Most brokers will allow you an initial interview, with no charge or commitment. The broker will need to ask you for details of your income and commitments, so that they can ascertain what is best for you – income, growth in the value of your initial investment or both. Taking into account your attitude to risk, they will advise you on which shares would best suit you. It is always a good idea to have researched some initial ideas yourself, so that you are better able to weigh-up and evaluate your broker's advice.

Portfolio management

Stockbrokers and independent financial advisers offer portfolio management services to individuals who prefer to hand over the responsibility for their investment decisions to professionals. Portfolio management is usually offered as a discretionary service. This means that once your investment objectives have been established, shares will be bought or sold on your behalf without you being consulted first – but you will be informed after each and every deal. You may need to have a certain size portfolio before a stockbroker will take you on – some firms stipulate a minimum of £100,000 – others may try and steer clients with less than, say, £50,000 into unit trusts instead of shares. But, as the APCIMS Directory shows, there are plenty of stockbrokers requiring far less than that – or no minimum at all. A portfolio management service could include annual valuations, advice on tax planning, regular stock market information, administrative paperwork and safe keeping of share certificates. The cost of these may be covered by an annual charge or by separate fees for each service you want.

Whatever service you opt for, make sure you understand the basis of charging and are absolutely clear whether the service is discretionary or non-discretionary.

How much does it cost?

In the main, stockbrokers make their living on the commission paid by clients when they buy and sell shares. Each firm will have its own rates based on the value of the 'parcel' of shares that is bought or sold at one time. There are no fixed rates, costs vary from firm to firm and there will probably be a minimum charge for small deals. Intermediaries such as

IFAs are entitled to add their own charge if they deal with a stockbroker on your behalf. Many stockbrokers still charge between 1 and 2 per cent to purchase shares of up to £5,000 in value but reduce the percentage commission on a sliding scale for larger amounts. Smaller purchases or sales may have a minimum charge – this could be between £10 and £35 or more. A larger minimum charge may suggest the stockbroker is not really interested in small investors – a lower minimum indicates the firm is keen and probably specializes in low-cost services for private investors. Increasingly, stockbrokers charge a flat fee whatever the size of the transaction.

Other share dealing charges are 0.5 per cent stamp duty (on purchase only) paid to the government *with a minimum charge of £5*. For all charges above this minimum, the rate of stamp duty will be rounded up to the nearest £5. For any transactions involving unit trusts, the original levy of £0.50 in every £100 still applies (£0.50 minimum charge). Your stockbroker will add this tax to the cost of any share that you buy. When share purchases are settled electronically within CREST (see next section) the transaction is liable to Stamp Duty Reserve Tax (SDRT). This is charged at an exact rate of 0.5 per cent (with no rounding up) of the initial purchase price. There is sometimes a compliance charge (which helps pay for the regulator). Once the deal is done, you will receive a contract note which you should keep carefully for your records.

Paying for shares

Most stock market transactions are settled three days after shares have been bought or sold. If you are sending a cheque by post, that can pose problems and there may be a penalty if the stockbroker receives payment late. Many stockbrokers accept payment by debit card over the phone. Alternatively you may set up an account with the firm so that money is already there to meet the cost of share purchases. Some stockbrokers will still give you ten days to pay following a transaction.

The London Stock Exchange system of settlement has recently undergone important changes. In the past the transfer and administration of share ownership involved a blizzard of paperwork for everyone. Now stock market transactions are done through an electronic system known as CREST which registers transfers.

As a result of these changes many investors find it more convenient to hold their shares through nominee accounts organized by their broker. If you hold your shares through a nominee account you are still the 'beneficial' owner of the shares and receive dividends but you do not receive share certificates and your name will not appear on the share register. Many investors find nominee accounts very convenient because their broker takes care of most of the paperwork. If you hold your shares through a nominee account you will not automatically get the company's annual reports, or invitations to its annual meeting where you have the right to vote, and you might lose your entitlement to shareholders' perks that may be offered by the companies you invest in. However, in many cases your broker will be able to arrange for you to participate fully as a shareholder and receive annual reports and other correspondence. If it is important to you that you receive this information, ensure that your broker will provide the service you need at a reasonable cost.

ProShare has devised a voluntary code of practice, the

ProShare Nominee Code, to which brokers and companies can sign up. Those brokers that adhere to the code are required to make their charges known fully, provide clear information about how investments held in their nominees are protected and to make arrangements, if asked, for the underlying investors to receive copies of annual reports and accounts of the companies whose shares are held (see pp. 48–58).

You can choose the traditional route, have your share certificates and be registered in your own name as a shareholder in the company, although it may involve an extra charge. You will have to keep your paperwork carefully.

There is another option. Active stock market investors can become sponsored members of CREST. As a sponsored member of CREST your shares will be held electronically, cutting out much of the paperwork but letting you keep all the rights of registered shareholders. There is an annual fee of £20 – but some stockbrokers may offer membership free. (Further details about nominee accounts and CREST can be found in ProShare's Investor Update 8 'What is a nominee?' and 9, 'How should I hold my shares?'. These free factsheets are available from ProShare's website at www.proshare.org.*)

You must agree the way in which you are going to hold your shares with whatever stockbroking service you choose.

The commission charge is not the only thing to look at when deciding who to deal with. A good broker may get you a better price for your shares, which can more than make up for his higher charges. Some brokers cut charges because they

---

*See **Chapter 16**, pp. 138–40, for a complete list of Investor Updates and details of how to obtain them.

do not carry out your order at once – and you may suffer for that delay.

If you opt for dealing with advice try to find out just how much attention you are going to get – a small country firm may be a better deal for the modest investor than a City one with lots of large clients and heavy overheads to cover.

Make sure you know the basis for charging right from the start – whether there is an annual charge, for instance.

Even if you opt for the discretionary portfolio, keep an eye on what is going on. Make sure you are not being traded in and out frequently (known as 'churning') and paying lots of commission to the broker, without much profit to you.

Your stockbroker may also be what is known as a 'market maker', meaning that they deal with shares on their own account and determine the price for that share according to supply and demand. A market maker should tell you when you are dealing in a share where his firm makes the market. That means he may be selling you shares his firm owns, or buying shares his firm wants itself. In some cases, this will mean you actually get a better deal. It should never mean that you get sold shares his firm wants to get rid of.

Beware too of independent financial advisers who ring regularly with suggestions of shares for you to buy. They may have bought a lot of them cheaply, and be selling them on to you at a higher price.

On-line services

If you decide to use a stockbroker offering an on-line service there are a number of additional things that you need to be aware of. Most Internet services now offer a 'deal at quote' system whereby you know exactly the price at which your shares will be bought or sold. Almost invariably, this type of service will require that you hold your shares in a nominee account. By accessing the broker's website address and keying in a password and security code (unique to each customer), you are able to buy or sell shares yourself. In reality, the brokerage firm still trades on your behalf. You will need to register with the broker and security checks will be carried out before you are able to trade. Current legislation requires that you sign an agreement with the broker before they can trade on your behalf. There is no electronic substitute for an ink signature yet!

The transaction will take place electronically, and the whole process happens in a fraction of the normal time. This should not be confused with 'on-line share ordering' which is carried out via e-mail. In this instance the private investor does not know the exact buying price when ordering, and will wait for the broker to contact him with these details before confirming the trade.

As with all broking services, the prices vary, so it pays to do your homework. Before you choose an on-line broker, make sure you are completely happy with the services you are buying into, and are clear about all the relevant charges you will incur. Remember also to check all the account conditions; some on-line brokers require a minimum balance, or a minimum initial deposit, before you can start using their services.

5

What Makes Share Prices Move?

Whether you are sizing up an individual share or looking at the market as a whole, it's most important to grasp one fundamental point: successful stock market investment is about anticipation and patience – assessing what is going to happen in six months, a year or five years from now. Understanding that is as important as keeping an eye on what is happening at the moment. This is one of the things that

baffles people about the stock market. When a company announces a big profits upturn it is often greeted with indifference by the stock market – the share price may even fall. This is because the increase in profits was anticipated and the share price had already risen: to use the jargon, the upturn was already 'in the price' and the market had already discounted the good results.

The professionals, the share analysts and fund managers will already be looking a year ahead. Is the company going to produce another spectacular rise in profits? Will there be a slowdown in growth? Even more confusingly, a share price might perk up after revealing poor profits or a loss. The thinking may be that the bad news is now out of the way, things are going to get better and now is the time to buy.

In Chapter 6 we will be looking at how you analyse individual shares. But first it is important to understand what influences the broad trend of the stock market. You don't have to be an economist – it's largely common sense.

Read the newspapers, particularly the financial press, on a regular basis and you will get a good idea of what people feel about the economy, where it is going, what the underlying economic trends are. All this influences the mood of the stock market.

When investors feel gloomy about the future, share prices tend to fall. It is what is known as a 'bear market'. When they feel prospects are good or improving, share prices tend to rise; this is a 'bull market'. These phases can last for several years although individual shares can 'buck the trend'. While it is certainly true that the stock market tends to amplify and exaggerate underlying trends, these movements are based on what investors believe is happening.

Interest rates are crucial, as we have seen all too clearly during periods when the high cost of finance has resulted in huge numbers of company and personal bankruptcies and falling profits and dividends. High interest rates slow down the economy, discourage consumers from spending and hit profits. One historical problem, however, has been that politicians have relied heavily on interest rates to alternatively perk up or slow down the UK economy.

Low interest rates stimulate the economy as companies are encouraged to invest and expand and consumers take advantage of cheaper credit – all of which helps corporate profits. Although the impact of lower interest rates will take some time to work through, share prices will start to anticipate the upturn in corporate profits well in advance. The stock market will get nervous when it sees interest rates rise.

The decision to give control of interest rates to the Bank of England has to some extent prevented the 'boom and bust' cycle we have experienced in the past. At the end of the day it is steady long-term growth in the economy that is good for investors, companies and employees alike.

Picking individual shares

When it comes to picking individual shares it's clear that some companies will benefit more, and sooner, than others from falling interest rates. If consumer spending looks as if it should pick up, the high-street retailers will be among the first to benefit, as will companies with large borrowings (so long as they are basically sound) – or industries like house building that are particularly sensitive to interest rates.

The trend in interest rates is also important when it comes to deciding what kind of investments you should hold. When interest rates are high, fixed-interest investments like gilt-edged securities can look more attractive than shares.

At a time when business and profits are going to be under pressure, a high fixed return looks a safe bet compared to the dividends on shares that, as we have seen, reflect the trend in company profits. When interest rates show signs of falling, on the other hand, the prospect of rising dividends and capital growth as the economy is stimulated makes shares far more attractive to investors seeking the best returns.

Shares can be a good way of protecting against inflation. Providing the economy is reasonably healthy, company profits and share dividends can keep abreast of or better inflation, providing growth in the value of your investment as well as providing income in the form of dividends. Whilst you can earn interest on a bank or building society account, the value of the capital may slowly be eroded by the impact of inflation.

Inflation is bad for the economy – and ultimately stock markets. Since the late 1970s and early 1980s when inflation reached 20 per cent at one point, governments have become very conscious of the need to keep it under control. The main way they have done this is by putting up interest rates and that can bring the economy juddering to a halt, with catastrophic results. In recent years, closer association with Europe has meant that interest rates have been relatively low and are likely to remain so.

Exchange rates are an important part of the investment scenario as well. Many major companies earn a substantial part of their profits abroad, providing investors with a spread of risk among a number of different economies. However, such companies are also susceptible to fluctuations in foreign exchange rates. Exchange rates also influence domestic economic policy.

For instance, our first ill-fated attempt to join the Exchange Rate Mechanism (ERM) designed to keep the EC currencies in line with each other resulted in a long period of high interest rates as we struggled to keep the pound within the ERM. That was disastrous for UK business.

A fall in the value of sterling against other international currencies, such as we experienced when we came out of the ERM in autumn 1992, is a mixed blessing. It makes British goods cheaper abroad, providing an initial boost to exports. On the other hand it puts up the price of imported goods and raw materials – so it can be inflationary as well.

When the value of sterling rises strongly in value compared with other currencies it is a problem for UK exporters, since it makes their goods look expensive to foreign consumers.

There are of course a host of other economic indicators which influence the stock market – and no two commentators will agree on the various implications. Stock markets are sensitive to political and international events – the short-term moves up and down can be alarming.

The UK stock market is influenced by what happens to other stock markets too. Remember the events of Black Monday in October 1987 when a huge fall on Wall Street on the previous Friday triggered off a similar collapse of share prices in London and other international stock markets.

But what investors should look at is the underlying trend. There is a mass of information published every day. What's happening in the high street – or increasingly over the Internet – are people buying? The retail sales statistics are published each month. What is business confidence like? The Confederation of British Industry (CBI) publishes regular surveys telling us what UK companies are thinking. Of course these indicators lag behind events and you need to look ahead.

Now consider the simplest share investment rule of all. **Buy when things appear gloomy.** Think about selling or switching investments when everyone thinks the boom is going to last forever. This is easier said than done, of course, and few investors are brave enough to buy right at the bottom and sell right at the top. But it illustrates the point that you need to use the information you have to anticipate what is going to happen in the longer term. And no one gets it right all of the time.

Trading systems

Two trading systems are currently operated by the London Stock Exchange. Traditionally, London has used a 'quote driven' system, where investors wishing to buy and sell particular shares approach a broker to ask the price quoted on SEAQ (the Stock Exchange Automated Quotations System) and to make the transaction on your behalf. The broker then buys the shares from a middleman known as a market maker. This system continues to be used for most shares outside the FTSE 100. You can either ask your broker to buy or sell shares 'at best' and he will buy or sell at the best price he can at the moment of the deal – which, given minute by minute price changes, may differ a little from his original quote. Your alternative is to set a limit on the price at which you want to buy or sell the shares. The stockbroker doesn't have to buy that day – he may allow you to leave the order for him to execute over the next few days if and when the price matches the limits you have given him, although not all brokers offer this service and some restrict the time period for which an order will stand to that particular trading day.

In 1997 a new 'order driven' system, SETS (the Stock Exchange Electronic Trading Service), changed the way in which shares in the largest 100 companies listed on the Stock

Exchange (FTSE 100 shares) and a few others are bought and sold. It is anticipated that more will be traded through the system in the future. Under the new system, you can place orders to buy and sell through your stockbroker who will then input your order on to an electronic order book to be matched. 'At best' orders are matched immediately at the best price on offer. 'Limit orders', which specify the worst price at which you wish the sale or purchase to take place, are matched in full or in part immediately, or sit on the order book and wait for a match and trade to result. For you as an investor there should not really be a noticeable difference between trading shares through either of the systems. One advantage is that limit orders are easier for brokers to transact using the order book. Most on-line broking services offer a 'deal at quote' system so that your deal is carried out immediately at the price given on screen.

When you are buying and selling by telephone, you should ask your stockbroker to repeat the instructions back to you, just to make sure they understand what you want. When trading on-line, there are a variety of things that you should watch out for. Before you click on the on-screen 'trade' instruction, read through the order carefully to make sure it is exactly what you want. Once a trade has been submitted on-line it is very difficult to change it as there is no delay in processing your order. If you have any concerns about a trade, call your broker to confirm the order. Another obvious mistake is to click the 'trade' instruction twice. Duplicate ordering is the single most common mistake made when trading on-line!

Bid, offer and spread

When you look at the share prices in the daily press you will see one price quoted. For shares outside the FTSE 100 it is usually the middle market price (i.e. the price midway between the last buying and last selling price) at the close of business the previous working day. For shares transacted through SETS it is usually the price at which the last trade on the previous day was transacted. It is not the price at which you can actually buy or sell the shares.

When you buy shares, you pay what is known as the offer price which is higher than the bid price that you will get if you sell them. The difference between the two prices is known as the spread. If you are buying shares in small or obscure companies you should check the size of the spread. If it's wider than average it could mean that the shares are not traded that frequently. When it comes to selling them you might find you get a poor price. This is often the case with penny shares.

Share prices can change frequently during the course of the day depending on how many are being bought and sold through the market. When there are more sellers than buyers, the prices will go down. When there are more buyers, the market will move prices up. It's a question of supply and demand – the fundamental rule of any market.

6

Looking at Individual Shares

There is a mass of information available on individual companies whose shares are quoted on the stock market. Stockbrokers produce regular reports, the financial pages of newspapers comment on results, specialist publications carry in-depth analyses, share tips (to be treated with caution) and profiles of the people running the companies. Many stockbrokers have monthly bulletins that they make available to their customers. These often make good reading and help enormously when it comes to picking and following shares.

The most comprehensive daily coverage of stock market and company matters in a national newspaper is found in the *Financial Times*, which also gives the fullest list of share prices and daily financial reports and information. Many investors just buy the Saturday edition of the *Financial Times* as it provides a comprehensive summary of the week's events on the stock market plus personal investment advice. It also lists directors' dealings in the shares of their own companies which many investors feel is a useful guide to prospects.

The *Investors' Chronicle* is a long-established weekly magazine aimed primarily at the private investor though it is read eagerly by City professionals as well. Other weekly titles include *Shares* magazine, which takes a down-to-earth approach to investment, and *Investors' Week*, with information for both private and professional investors. These titles all give comprehensive information on financial and economic events and issues. There is also useful coverage of company news and results, statistical information and comment on individual companies.

Aside from the *Financial Times*, there is daily financial and business news coverage in most national and some regional newspapers, though some have larger sections than others. If you invest in AIM or smaller company shares you might not find much relevant information on a regular basis. Most newspapers carry ever-larger personal finance sections – usually on Saturday and Sunday – but the coverage of individual shares, as opposed to unit and investment trusts, for instance, tends to be patchy. This is not surprising because the major fund management and insurance companies are very big advertisers in these sections.

Some newspapers do feature share-tipping columns or personal stock market diaries on a regular basis. How investors should respond to them is a controversial matter. Look at their track record. What has happened to past suggestions? It's all very well if a share goes up immediately after it has been tipped in the press. But has it sustained and increased its price after that? It may well be a mistake to buy a share on a Monday that has been tipped at the weekend because there will be lots of demand for the share and the price might be temporarily inflated. You may get a better price a few days later. Share-tipping columns are worth reading because they provide a point of view – with which you can agree or disagree – and plenty of ideas. They are not gospel, but can be a useful way for a novice stock market investor to familiarize him or herself with the stock market even if you don't decide to follow their suggestions.

There are also plenty of investment newsletters around, sold on subscription. Many of them specialize in small company, high technology or AIM shares, and they can be very informative and useful. But subscribing to one or more of these can represent a major investment in itself, though you may often see special offers for, say, a three-month trial advertised in the newspapers.

In the not-too-distant past, private investors did not have access to all the instant data available to City professionals, and the electronic news and share price services available in City offices are simply too expensive for the individual. The advent of the Internet has revolutionized the way in which private investors can access information. There is now a variety of Internet services and affordable computer software packages that enable investors to access stock market data through their personal computers. A multitude of investment websites have sprung up recently offering excellent up-to-date news, shares prices and portfolio management tools for the private investors, putting them on an equal footing with City professionals.

Portfolio management/analysis systems are offered by many sites, and it is worth spending some time researching these to find out what is on offer and which one best suits your needs. In many cases you will find that these sites are free of charge. Particular things to watch out for are how often the information is updated, whether they offer a news summary or customer support, and whether they offer more complex services like tax and transaction summaries and share analysis data programmes. Sites often offer share data, the main advantage of which for investors is that share prices quoted on-line are often real-time; which means that the price given is the current market price. If prices are not real-time, an on-screen disclosure will advise users of the last time the price was updated. Other prices may be listed as delayed (usually by about fifteen minutes), end of day, or historical (going back several months or more).

The best way to search for investment websites is to use an Internet directory. There are a number of directories to choose from, many with exotic names such as Yahoo, Lycos and Excite. As the name suggests, an Internet directory is an attempt to categorize services under meaningful topics. Subjects such as entertainment, motoring, and the media may well be covered, as will areas such as business, finance and investment. Once you have selected your directory (and have chosen the topic) simply type in a word or phrase that best describes what you are looking for, and click on 'search'. If, for example, you are looking for on-line brokerage firms try typing in 'on-line stockbrokers' or 'on-line trading' and see what the search brings up. Some useful sites are:

www.ftyourmoney.com

www.moneyguru.com

www.ukinvest.co.uk

www.hemscott.net

www.fool.co.uk

www.ftmarketwatch.com

www.digitallook.com

www.londonstockexchange.co.uk

www.iii.co.uk

ProShare's website www.proshare.org has lots of useful information and contains Investor Update 5 'Where to get investment information' which provides further details.*

Additionally you can access daily financial news highlights free of charge through Ceefax and Teletext, which also have regularly updated share prices available.

Much more elaborate – and much more expensive – are the company information services aimed at the private investor. The most comprehensive is probably *Company REFS* by HS Financial which is available on either a monthly or quarterly basis either in a CD ROM or paper format (available at some libraries). Pioneered by stock market guru Jim Slater, the service covers virtually all stock market companies, including those traded on AIM. The wealth of financial and investment statistics means it is probably too sophisticated for the novice investor, but if you get hooked on stock market investment it is a valuable tool. In addition, its sister company, hemscott.net, provides a useful service for investors where, if you use them as your Internet service provider (ISP), you gain access to free information including five-year price histories, brokers' forecasts, directors' share-dealings, up-to-the-minute financial news and alerts, and expert company analysis.

ProShare's publication, *The Investor's Guide to Information Sources* takes the effort out of tracking down the most useful sources of information from so many different places. It also has a new expanded Internet section. It includes a summary of contents, a rating and a ProShare comment on each information source featured.**

*See **Chapter 16**, pp. 138–40, for a complete list of Investor Updates.
See **Chapter 16, pp. 136–7, for details of this and other ProShare publications.

Reading company reports

More and more publicly quoted companies are realizing the value of having their own website. It is an ideal way to communicate up-to-the-minute news and financial information and goes a long way towards answering private investors' complaints that they do not have the same privileges as City professionals. Currently all FTSE 100 companies have dedicated sites and the proportion of companies in the rest of the stock market going on-line grows daily, though the standard of information and presentation varies enormously.

Amongst this information is likely to be an on-line version of the company's annual report and accounts. Whether in hard copy or electronic format, these are often complex documents which must comply with certain legal requirements. Yet the information they contain can be crucial if you are thinking of investing in a particular company. Many company reports look like glossy magazines, so full of photographs that it gets confusing. Others may be quite austere.

Whatever the presentation there are key features, common to all, that you should consider. It is always best to look at companies with a track record of at least five years and look at the trends over this time. You should be looking for companies that will perform over the long term and give you a portfolio of sound shares that will rise steadily in value. Most report and accounts now contain a five-year summary of a company's key financial statistics.

Profit and loss account

This tells you how well (or badly) the company traded during the year – how much profit it made and how much dividend it is paying. This will be shown side by side with the results for the previous year so you can make a comparison. Most of the important information on profits will already have been included in the preliminary statement, which is normally made available a few weeks before the publication of the annual report and accounts. The preliminary statement is released to the London Stock Exchange and the press, but not normally posted to shareholders, although changes to Company Law are afoot that may alter this. It gives the results for the year, but the annual report will give you a much fuller picture of what a company has been doing.

Profit and Loss Account

For Year Ended 31 December 1999	Notes	Current year £000s	Previous year £000s
Turnover	1	150,000	100,000
less Cost of sales	2	(116,500)	(84,800)
equals **Operating profit (before tax)**		33,500	15,200
plus Net interest	3	200	150
equals **Pre-tax profit on ordinary activities**		33,700	15,350
less Extraordinary items	4	(2,000)	(1,000)
equals **Profit for the financial year**		31,700	14,350
less Taxation	5	(10,650)	(5,160)
equals **Profit after taxation**		21,050	9,190
less Minority interests	6	(200)	(150)
equals **Profit attributable to ordinary shareholders**		20,850	9,040
less Dividends	7	(10,300)	(5,000)
equals **Profit retained in the business**		10,550	4,040
Earnings per share		6.1	3.0

Sales

Turnover means the amount of goods or services a company has sold. The annual report should disclose some interesting additional information – the proportion of sales overseas, for instance, and which divisions of the business are more important or achieved a better performance than others. You should look at the half-year interim results as well when you assess sales performance. Maybe sales slowed in the second half – maybe they are increasing faster. Obviously, retailers do most of their business over Christmas and the New Year. The annual sales figure is not necessarily the whole picture.

If you look at the company's sales over five years, you should be able to see whether the company has been increasing its business in recent times. To assess the trading profit – how much a company is making from its actual business – you have to look at the operating profit. Cost of sales and other expenses tell you how much a company has spent on running the business and is a rough but useful guide to efficiency. If costs are rising in relation to sales, that could be a warning – or indicate an area that could improve with better management. This includes the major item of wage costs – though details will also be shown separately elsewhere in the accounts. It may also include depreciation, the amount set aside to cover the wear and tear on plant and machinery. In theory, depreciation builds up a fund to cover the cost of buying new machinery when it is needed. Often there are numbered 'notes' to the accounts which include more information on specific items and provide more detail.

Profits

Pre-tax profit is a crucial figure – the one that is widely
regarded as the leading indicator of a company's performance. A good indicator is when the pre-tax profits have been
increasing steadily over time. Before that figure is struck,
the profit and loss account will show net interest which is
worth looking at carefully. If a company has a lot of cash
and few borrowings, interest received should exceed interest
payments resulting in a plus for net interest. For most companies, interest paid will be greater than interest earned
causing a charge against profits. For businesses with heavy
borrowings, movements in interest rates are an important
factor when it comes to assessing future profits. If interest
costs are way up, it could mean the company has more
borrowings and overdrafts – or that interest rates have been
much higher.

The results of many companies will include adjustments
for exceptional items – unusual gains and losses made during
the year which are not part of normal trading activities. These
might include profits from selling a factory or some other
asset, the losses on closing a business and making redundancy
payments, or the gain from selling a subsidiary company.
These items are shown separately in the profit and loss
account so everyone can see them clearly, and understand
what they mean.

Deductions and dividends

Tax is the next major item. Profits after tax or profit from the
financial year show you what the company made from its
year's trading after all costs, charges and deductions. This is
what the company earned. After deducting any preference

dividends, this is the figure used to calculate the earnings per share.

A steadily increasing earnings per share figure is a good sign of a growing company. It is also needed to arrive at the price/earnings ratio – the important investment yardstick described in Chapter 3 (pp. 21–3).

Minority interests may figure next. These cover the profits or losses from businesses which the main company does not own completely, so part of the profit or loss belongs to outside shareholders. If that business is making a profit, the minority interest will be a deduction from the main company's profit. If it is losing money, then the minority shareholder has to bear part of the loss, so the minority interest will show up as a plus in the main company's figures.

Some of the post-tax profit will be distributed as dividends to ordinary shareholders. The rest, shown as profit retained in the business at the bottom of the profit and loss account, will remain in the business and become part of the assets shown in the balance sheet, which is the next item in the annual report that investors should consider.

Balance sheet

The balance sheet is not an infallible guide to a company's financial health. It shows what a company owns and owes on the last day of its financial year. You can be sure that it tries to look its best! None the less, it is important to understand what the items in the balance sheet mean – how they can highlight a company's strengths and weaknesses. A specimen balance sheet is shown over.

Specimen Balance Sheet			
Balance Sheet as at December 1997	Notes	Current year £000s	Previous year £000s
Fixed assets			
Land and buildings		5,000	3,000
Plant and machinery		20,000	15,000
Total fixed assets		25,000	18,000
Current assets			
Cash at bank		2,000	2,000
Debtors		15,000	12,000
Stocks		12,500	10,000
Investments		5,000	4,000
less			
Current liabilities			
amounts due within one year		(14,000)	(12,000)
equals			
Net current assets		20,500	16,000
Total net assets		45,500	34,000
Shareholders' funds			
Share capital		34,950	29,960
Retained profits		10,550	4,040
		45,500	34,000

The first item is fixed assets – what the company owns in the way of land, property, factories, machinery, etc. It is worth looking at the valuation for properties. If they haven't been re-valued for years they might be worth far more at present-day values.

Current assets include the company's stocks, cash investments and money owed by debtors. The figure for stocks is very important – if that moves significantly out of line with sales you might wonder why. A big increase might suggest that sales are not on target, the company has miscalculated demand, or it might mean that there are teething problems with a new distribution system. It costs the company money to hold stock.

It is always comforting to find plenty of cash or near cash in the balance sheet. As with the profit and loss account you can make a comparison and look for trends in the previous years. Movements in cash balances are also analysed in the cash flow statement – described below.

Current liabilities include the company's short-term borrowings – those it has to pay back within a year – and money it owes to suppliers and other creditors. High short-term borrowings might be a worry – particularly if the company's current assets do not include much cash. Running out of cash to pay the bills is how companies go bust, never mind how sound the assets may look.

After deducting these and other liabilities, like long-term bank loans, from the assets, the balance sheet gives a figure for net assets – what would theoretically be left to distribute to shareholders if the company sold everything and paid its debts.

When stock market professionals talk about 'asset backing', they mean how much these assets are worth per share. But as we have seen, it is important to study the balance sheet to see how the assets are made up and what they might really be worth. Clearly it is more interesting from the investment angle if much of the asset value lies in cash or near cash or very saleable land or property. It is not so exciting if it is all in ancient plant or machinery, which often may be worth less than it seems.

Watch out for gearing

Assets and liabilities make up one side of the balance sheet whilst shareholders' funds make up the other side. These comprise share capital, reserves and the undistributed profits of the business built up over the years. This is effectively the money that finances the business. A key point to watch is the proportion of borrowings to shareholders' funds – known as 'gearing' by the professionals. Acceptable gearing levels vary from business to business, but anything over 50 per cent should be viewed carefully. It could mean a chunk of profits will be gobbled up by interest charges.

Examine cash flows

The annual accounts will also include a cash flow statement – this is an important part of share analysis. It shows you how cash has come into the business over the year – and what use has been made of it. Cash is generated mainly from trading profits – but there may be sales of assets as well, or new share issues. It will show how this cash was spent – on buying assets and paying tax and dividends. The point of this statement is to see if the company has a good cash flow (hopefully the amount of money coming in will match or exceed the amount going out). By looking at the changes in items like stocks and bank balances shown here you can learn a lot about the way a business is being run, whether it has sufficient working capital.

Don't forget the Notes

Much of the substance relating to the profit and loss account and the balance sheet will actually be in the notes to the accounts. It is important to read these carefully. Before you do, take a few minutes to wade through the statement of accounting policies. It may appear hard-going. But as you become more accustomed to accounts, you will begin to see that this can sometimes be crucial. It effectively defines what the figures really mean. Pay extra attention to any change in accounting policies from the previous year. There will be a good reason for it – and do not necessarily assume that, if some phrase is missing one year, it has been left out by chance.

In their report, the auditors state whether, in their opinion, the annual accounts comply with the law and give shareholders a true and fair view of the state of the company. Sometimes, however, auditors' reports are qualified – usually because the auditors do not agree with some of the accounting methods used. It is especially worrying when the auditors make reference to matters affecting the ability of the company to continue as a going concern. That means that the company has financial difficulties and could go bust unless its bankers, or other lenders, continue to support it.

The company will be well into its next financial year by the time the annual report and accounts is published, so the chairman's statement may contain some information on current trading – and more may be revealed at the annual general meeting. Shareholders can go to that – and ask questions if they wish.

The report of the directors will give you information about any changes in company business or structure and will show the board members' own shareholdings in the company and the names of anyone else with more than 3 per cent. It also tells you about any options the directors have been given to buy shares. This is a useful way of boosting their rewards from the company. A reasonable options policy, when directors seem to have sufficient incentives, though payments are not of 'fat cat' standards, can be good for both board and shareholders.

ProShare's *Introduction to Annual Reports and Accounts* is a simple guide to the main features in a company's reports and accounts, explaining what to look out for and how to interpret the information, including a guide to financial jargon.*

*See **Chapter 16**, p. 138, for details of this guide and how to order it.

7

What's a Share Worth?

Open the *Financial Times* at the prices pages and you will quickly see that there are hundreds of shares to choose from. Many other newspapers also contain such financial information. Look more closely and each day there will be some clear winners and a few nasty losers. The key to successful investment is telling one from another, but before you can do that you need to be able to understand what all those columns of figures on the prices pages are telling you.

Vital statistics

Pick any share. Going left to right across the columns you will find the previous day's middle market price (explained in Chapter 5, p. 42). Then there is a column that shows you how the price moved since the close of the market on the previous trading day – by how much it was up or down.

Then it gives you the highs and lows for the last twelve months – you can see how much it has moved up and down.

Next you will find the trading volume rounded to the nearest 1,000 trades. This shows how many shares in this company were traded in the last day that the market was open. A dash indicates that no trade took place or the information is

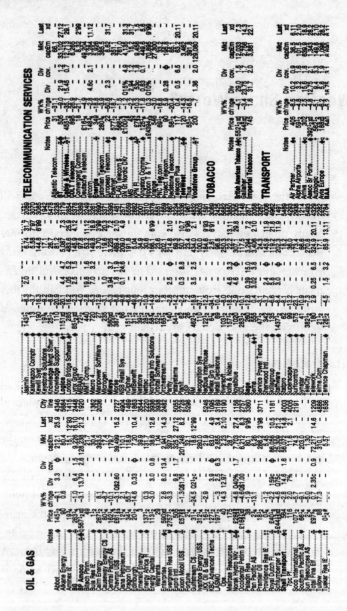

OIL & GAS

TELECOMMUNICATION SERVICES

TOBACCO

TRANSPORT

not available. A zero indicates that less than 500 trades took place.

Then you have the dividend yield. This shows the percentage return on the share before income tax is deducted. It is calculated by dividing the gross dividend by the current share price and multiplying the result by 100.

The final column shows the price/earnings ratio (usually referred to as the p/e ratio) – the other important investment yardstick explained in Chapter 3.

Stock market sectors

All shares are grouped under a particular sector. If you look at the prices pages you will see a long list – textiles, property, hotels and leisure, food manufacturing, etc. It helps you find the price you want more quickly. Grouping companies into sectors provides an important tool for comparing the share price performance of different companies. Next, turn to the stock market report page in the *Financial Times*. There you will find a table of the FTSE indices.

FTSE indices

The FTSE 100 Share Index is the most widely used barometer of stock market ups and downs. It reflects the combined performance of the shares of the 100 largest companies listed on the London Stock Exchange.

There are other indices as well. The FTSE 250 charts the combined performance of the next 250 largest stock market companies below the top 100, while the FT Actuaries All Share Index shows the daily performance of the top 800 companies. It is a broader measure of stock market movements. It forms the basis for the whole series of indices which reflect the price movements of shares in different sectors.

Sector indices

Indices like the FTSE 100 show you what the stock market is doing overall. But within that, shares in the various industrial groups may follow a different pattern. That is reflected in the various sector indices, which show the average movement of shares in that sector plus the sector's average dividend yield and p/e ratio.

All these different indices help investors to decide whether an individual share is worth buying, if it's time to sell and how well their portfolio is doing against the stock market as a whole.

Relative performance

As you begin to follow the stock market more closely you will find that the professionals talk a lot about the 'relative performance' of shares as well as the overall trend. You will hear phrases such as 'this share is undervalued' or 'that share is overvalued'. Different sectors and companies may be 'due for a re-rating'. The shrewd investor wants to buy shares that are likely to outperform the rest of the stock market – that is, do better relative to the rest. The various indices we have outlined above act as benchmarks by which to assess individual share performance – and can help pin-point shares that may outperform the rest of the stock market.

Say you spot a share in the food-retailing sector. You have looked at the accounts and decided that it is a good or growing business. But before you buy you want to find out a bit more about the likely performance of the shares.

Price/earnings ratio

Is the price/earnings (p/e) ratio high or low compared with the sector average? It's low. That is interesting, but it does not mean that the shares are undervalued. A lower than average p/e ratio can indicate a number of things.

It might mean profits are expected to be down this year – when you work out the p/e ratio on the basis of reduced earnings per share you may find it's bang on the average. Or it could mean that even if profits are growing they may be doing so at a slower rate than other food retailers. The company may be small and therefore considered more vulnerable. Compare the market capitalization with the higher-rated companies in the sector as bigger companies may command a higher p/e ratio.

That is not to say the shares are not worth buying. It merely demonstrates that the p/e ratio reflects what the stock market feels about the shares. It is not expecting particularly scintillating profits growth. But feelings can change – so can companies.

If the company is entering a period of above-average

profits growth then there may indeed be a 're-rating' of the shares in the future – this is the sort of thing every investor hopes to stumble on.

Maybe the share you fancy has a high p/e ratio relative to the sector. This does not mean it is overvalued – it usually reflects the fact that the company has had consistently higher than average profits and earnings growth – so far. What you have to judge is whether this is going to continue. Shares get re-rated down as well as up and a high relative p/e ratio makes them very vulnerable if profits fall short of expectations.

The private investor has to bear in mind the massive amount of research that goes on in the City. Stockbrokers' analysts and institutional investors are well-placed to keep an eye on what is happening to leading companies. It's unlikely for instance that you will come across a seriously undervalued blue chip share that no one else has spotted – the analysts monitor these companies very closely.

The different sectors, and the major companies within them, respond to shifts in the economic cycle. At the first sign of a recovery you might find that retail shares and house-building shares are among the first to start moving upwards as the stock market anticipates a rise in consumer spending. That may be followed by a rise in the share prices of companies that supply the stores and make building materials – and so will benefit from increased demand.

There may be a fashion for certain industries, often new ones, which look as if they are going to grow very fast over the next few years. The sector indices are a useful tool that show you what the stock market feels about that particular industrial grouping. Combined with your own judgement about future economic trends it helps you decide if it is likely to underperform or outperform the stock market.

In Chapter 3 we suggested that you pick a few shares for a hypothetical portfolio – monitoring them to see how they perform. If sufficient time has passed, compare your portfolio as a whole with the FTSE 100 Index – would your shares have done better, worse, or kept up with the stock market average over the last few months?

Then have a look at each individual share. Did it respond to general news on the economy in the way you expected? How did it respond if any results have been announced meanwhile? Now you have much more knowledge about the way the stock market works and values shares. Apply that to your hypothetical portfolio. Why have some shares done better than others? Are your original assumptions proving correct? Think about it carefully.

ProShare has developed a system to make the process of analysing shares more simple and improving your ability to compare like with like. The system is explained below, and then covered in more detail in Chapter 14, Your Share Portfolio.

How to analyse a share

Making use of some of the principles we have already talked about to evaluate a share, ProShare has developed a unique system which can be used by investors, whether experienced or complete newcomers, to help them choose successful shares – those that have a good performance record, a bright future and that are on offer at an attractive price.

The system is based on four basic principles:

You should buy shares in a company with a proven track record

The main bulk of your portfolio should be made up of six to twelve companies about which you are so confident that, unless a major change occurs, you will be happy to own them for at least the next five years.

Invest regularly and ignore market ups and downs

If you invest what you can afford at regular intervals you are bound to benefit because long-term the overall trend of the stock market has always been upwards.

Reinvest your dividends

This is called compounding and you will be surprised at the difference this makes to the overall performance of your portfolio.

Don't put all your eggs in one basket

It is important to spread risk and opportunity across different companies in terms of company size and stock market sector.

Although there is a place in your portfolio for some more risky investments, the basis of your investment portfolio should be made up of companies that have demonstrated over time their ability to achieve good results. Well-established companies have experience and have shown that they can make profits for themselves and their shareholders.

Do you understand the company?

One of the first rules of investment is to understand the companies that you invest in. You need to know what the business you are considering investing in does and what the implications are of decisions made by the management.

If you really understand what the company does, then ask

yourself whether the product or service in which the company specializes is likely to bring in profits in the future. Consider likely threats and competitors and whether customers are likely to continue to buy. Does the company have a good reputation for quality and value? It is always a good idea to talk to people who know about the kind of business you are looking at and get their thoughts about the company. You should also comb the financial pages of the newspapers and the other publications for news, check on the Internet, visit the reference library and send for the annual report for news and comment.

Does the company have a good track record?

The company should have a good track record over recent years – it is sensible to look back at least five years. You should look at past turnover and check whether the profits have been increasing year after year. The company should be getting better and better at what it does and so customers should be buying more and more. Of course it is no guarantee of what is going to happen in the future, but it is facts like these that establish what the company is worth and help its share price to go up.

It is important that the company's sales, profits, dividends and share price are increasing steadily as unpredictable ups and downs in turnover and profits bring their own management and cash flow problems. It is also important to check that the current share price is good value for money. You might identify the best company in the world, but if the current share price is too high it is not the right time to buy. Prices go up and down all the time, so wait until the price is right.

Keep track of what the experts are saying about the company. City analysts dedicate their careers to assessing and monitoring companies so you should value their expert opinion in predicting a company's future accurately. Find out what the analysts are thinking before making up your own mind.

Ensure that you thoroughly research all aspects of a company you are considering investing in – never buy on a whim or without knowing all the facts.

Profits for the shareholders

We saw before that pre-tax profits are a leading indicator of a company's performance and again you are looking for a steady upwards trend.

Once tax has been deducted, the earnings per share or EPS figure can be calculated and, once again, we're looking for a steadily increasing figure over five years.

Is the management effective?

The best way of assessing the effectiveness of the management of a business is by comparing the profits with the turnover. If the business brought in £100m and the operating profit – that's the profit before tax and interest have been deducted – is £10m then the operating margin is 10 per cent. Generally, a reasonable operating margin is a good thing as it indicates that the management are getting a good price for what they are selling. However, watch out if the operating margin seems extremely high compared to other companies in the same business. It could be a sign that the company is making excessive profits and competitors may undercut them.

It is also useful to calculate the return on capital employed (ROCE) as this gives an indication of all the return the company is making on all the money tied up in the business. For this calculation you need to divide the pre-tax profit by the money used to finance the business including shares in issue and any loans taken out by the company.

Again, a reasonable to high ROCE figure is good news. It means that a better-than-average amount of profit is being made available to the business. Consistently improving operating margins and ROCE are a good indication that the company is being managed efficiently.

Is the share good value for money today?

To decide whether today's share price is good value for money, look at the price movements over recent years, the money the company has earned for the shareholders in earnings per share (EPS) and the p/e ratio.

First look at the share price itself and the high and low share prices in the previous five years. How does the current price compare? Has the share price been volatile during this time? The p/e ratio as we have seen before represents the number of years it would take you to get back the costs of your investment, assuming that the price and the profits stayed the same. It's a good guide to what other investors think the company is worth, so if you compare today's p/e ratio with that average over the last few years you can easily work out whether you might be looking at a bargain or an overpriced share.

Look also at the company's current p/e ratio compared to others in its sector to see whether it is higher or lower than the average. Look also at the sector's average p/e ratio and see how it compares with p/e ratios of other sectors to see whether the sector is in favour or not.

Should you be buying this share?

If you are satisfied that you understand what this company does and are sure that its customers will continue to want its products and services, rather than those of its competitors, for years to come, then it is worth considering the company. If the company's sales and profits record and the EPS are growing steadily and the share price and its movements seem to indicate the price is undervalued at the moment, then now might be the time to buy.

If in one year, there's a blip in the progress of the figures, then it is imperative to find out why. You can't afford to ignore it. Get the annual reports, find out what the problem was. Was it serious? Is it likely to recur? Did the chairman or the Chief Executive say what had caused the problem and – more important – what are they doing to make sure it doesn't happen again?

If there is more than one blip, it could be serious. Unless the reasons and remedies are satisfactorily explained to you, our advice is to forget this company. There are plenty of other, blipless, companies to choose from.

Other checks include looking at directors' dealings in shares of their own companies. Do they collectively own a substantial number of the shares and are they recent buyers or sellers?

You have identified the reasons for the company's success. Are they strong enough to ensure its future prosperity or do you know of another ingredient that will boost the profits? If you have any uncertainties at all – do not buy. In investing it is always better to be safe than sorry.

8

Collective Investments

Many investors get their first taste of the stock market through buying unit trusts. These funds, which you will see advertised and written about in the personal finance pages of the national press, are a good alternative if you don't feel confident enough to pick your own shares, or if you want a broader spread of investments to balance a small equity portfolio. But buying unit trusts is not a way of avoiding having to use your own investment judgement. With well over 1,000 funds on the market – some of them highly specialized – picking the right one requires some serious homework.

What is a unit trust?

A unit trust is a fund that invests in shares. When you buy 'units' you are acquiring not the underlying shares but a stake in the whole fund that will own many holdings in different companies quoted on the stock market. A unit trust's investments are looked after by professional managers who decide which shares to buy and sell. Unit trusts are often described as 'open ended'. As investors buy units, the size of the fund increase as it has more money to invest. If they sell units, the underlying investments can be sold. In practice, in normal markets there is a two-way traffic in units. Your stockbroker or financial adviser will be happy to make recommendations and buy the units for you. You can also buy units through a discount broker where you may find you get a better deal on units as they will reimburse all or part of your commission.

Unit trusts versus shares

Over the last thirty years unit trusts have been very popular with investors – even at times when fewer private individuals were buying individual shares. One of their main advantages is that they offer the small investors a good spread of investments at a reasonable cost.

Say you have £1,000 to put into the stock market. Because you have to pay a minimum commission each time you deal through a stockbroker, it will be expensive for you to buy more than a couple of different shares. Maybe you are nervous about putting all the money in one or two companies. You might buy a unit trust instead – that will give you a stake in the wider range of stock market companies and you won't have to pay several lots of commission.

Unit trusts have another important advantage – they offer

you an easy way of investing abroad. Buying individual shares in overseas companies is a bit daunting – but there are strong arguments for having some part of your investments in overseas stock markets. You would find it difficult to get into the Far Eastern stock markets, for instance, in any other way.

The major disadvantage is that putting all your portfolio into unit trusts takes a lot of the fun out of choosing your own stock market investments. And because funds invest in many different companies, no unit trust is likely to equal the performance of one real stock market winner – or indeed a real stock market disaster.

Picking unit trusts

There are so many funds that this is almost as tricky as picking shares. A number of publications including *The Investor*, *What Investment* and *Money Management* carry articles, details of what is available and performance statistics. Many finance websites carry information and www.trustnet.co.uk is dedicated to the subject of collective investments.

Funds are divided into a number of different sectors and even if you just want to buy into the British stock market there are a baffling number – growth funds, income funds, smaller company funds. There are international funds with shares in many overseas stock markets – and unit trusts that invest in just one region – North America for instance, or Japan. There are the highly specialized funds investing in gold shares, or property – or recovery funds where the managers select shares that have had a bad time but which they believe will now do well. There are unit trusts that invest in other unit trusts within the same investment management group – these are known as 'funds of funds'. How on earth do you start? As with buying shares, you have to decide what kind of investment or combination of investments you are looking for.

If you want long-term capital growth, look first at the UK general and UK growth unit trusts. These make a sensible basis for any unit trust portfolio. Pick a broad-based fund that has performed well and steadily over the last few years. These funds will rarely feature among the top industry performers. But if you want a solid investment this is where you should start.

If income is important to you, there are plenty of UK equity income unit trusts that invest in shares with above average yields – and give you capital growth as well.

International unit trusts are a good way to get a stake in a wide range of overseas stock markets. It means that your portfolio is not entirely dependent on what happens at home.

One country or region funds are another possibility. Through these you can invest in emerging markets or in developed economies like Japan, North America and Europe. But you should be aware that exchange rates can have a big impact on the value of your investments too. This is particularly important if you invest in one country or region.

Like shares, unit trusts should be considered as long-term investments, making up the core of your portfolio. More active investors, who are prepared to take a greater risk with part of their money, should look at the specialist unit trusts on offer.

You will find recovery funds in the UK growth sector. Managers of these will be looking for 'bombed out' shares with recovery potential – particularly interesting as the economy climbs out of recession.

UK smaller companies are another, more volatile sector.

These often do well in the final stages of a stock market boom.

Other cyclical sectors that you can invest in through unit trusts include property and gold shares.

Remember that the narrower the investment range the more volatile the fund can be. With these specialist funds, timing is all important. If you manage to buy at the bottom and sell at the top you can make handsome profits. Get it wrong and you can make hefty losses. You must know about the sector, be prepared to take a bit of a gamble – and be ready to sell if you think it the right thing to do. Above all, don't commit more than a small proportion of your portfolio to this kind of fund.

Costs

The cost of investing in a unit trust is included in the initial price you pay for your 'units'. You usually pay a front end charge of around 5 per cent which covers the manager's own dealing expenses, and commission. In addition an annual management charge of between 0.75 per cent and 1.5 per cent is paid to the fund manager. It is a mistake to assume that it is always cheaper to buy unit trusts rather than shares – much depends on the size and spread of your personal portfolio.

Open Ended Investment Companies

Open Ended Investment Companies (OEICs) are similar to unit trusts because the fund can increase or reduce the number of units depending on the demand from investors. OEICs (pronounced 'Oicks') are relatively new here but have long been popular in Europe. The main difference is that they are companies, not trusts, and there is just one price at which investors both buy and sell the 'units'. Units can be bought direct from the OEIC manager, or through a third party such as a stockbroker or independent financial adviser.

Investment trusts

Like unit trusts, investment trusts offer investors a way of spreading their stock market risks through pooled or collective investment. Like unit trusts, investment trusts manage a portfolio of shares and also offer a convenient route to overseas stock markets. And again like unit trusts, investment trusts offer a good range of investment possibilities – from reliable general funds covering the whole of the stock market to more specialist categories of investment. But there are important differences.

Investment trusts are companies that have shares that are quoted on the stock market. What determines the price of those shares is not only the value of their underlying portfolio as in the case of unit trusts, but the demand for them on the stock market. This complication explains why they have not, until recently, been so popular with small investors. The price of a unit trust 'unit' directly reflects the stock market value of the trust's portfolio of underlying shares. An investment trust share, on the other hand, usually sells at a discount to the value of its portfolio. The size of this discount can vary. That introduces an element of uncertainty into the investment equation. When investment trust shares were out of fashion a few years ago, the discounts grew very large – a third or more. Nowadays they are much smaller, reflecting their increasing popularity with investors.

Naturally, the shares of well-managed trusts where the fund managers have increased the value of their portfolio by skilful investment are in demand – the shares will go up as the value of the portfolio rises. In addition, the discount will narrow, so there is a double gain. Obviously the discount means there is an element of extra risk, too – discounts can widen as well as shrink. Investment trust shares do broadly follow the progress of their underlying share portfolios. And they have some advantages over unit trusts.

Investment trusts can borrow money to invest. This 'gearing' gives investors greater growth potential – and higher risks. They can also invest in unquoted companies although these can be riskier investments. Investment trusts can be attractive take-over targets when their assets are worth substantially more than the market value of their shares.

Split-capital investment trusts are specialist investments offering different kinds of shares depending on whether the investor wants capital growth or income. In simple terms all the income from the shares in the trust go to one class of shareholder while the capital growth goes to another. These kind of investment trusts have a definite winding-up date when the underlying investments can be sold. These are sophisticated investments with varying share structures. Potential investors should take advice from a stockbroker or IFA before buying. Investment trusts have lower management charges, as a rule, than unit trusts. The bid/offer spread (i.e. the difference between the buying and selling price) for a large trust may be less than 3 per cent. Shares are bought through the stock market – on larger amounts commission costs can be lower than buying a comparable unit trust.

Your stockbroker will certainly be able to give you advice on what to buy. Again, *What Investment*, *The Investor* and *Money Management* publish performance tables and commentary and www.trustnet.co.uk provides a variety of information, including performance tables. As with unit trusts, your choice boils down to defining your investment profile and what kind of funds, or mixture of funds, are suitable for you. The same general rules apply.

Regular savings schemes for unit and investment trusts

Many unit and investment trusts offer regular savings schemes which is a useful way of building up capital if you don't have a lump sum to invest. Many of these schemes offer minimum monthly investments of as little as £50 or less, making them simple and cost-effective for first-time investors. To make things easier, the shares from these savings schemes are held in a nominee and regular statements are sent to you. You can also invest in them through an ISA. The Association of Unit Trusts and Investment Funds and The Association of Investment Trust Companies have helpful leaflets for potential investors.*

*See **Chapter 16, Useful Addresses** (pp. 141–2), for contact telephone numbers/website addresses.

9

A Beginner's Guide to Gilts

Shares are not the only kind of investment traded on the stock market. Government securities – or gilts as they're known – account for a large slice of daily market activity. But what are gilts? How do they differ from shares? What part can they play in your investment portfolio?

Gilts are a form of government borrowing. Selling gilts is one of the ways in which government raises money to fund its spending programme. They are sometimes called government bonds.

Gilts are always traded in units of £100 nominal (or face) value. They offer investors a fixed interest return – in the form of twice-yearly payments – and the promise of repayment of the nominal capital at a specified date. But it is important to understand that, while government backing makes them secure investments with a certain and quantifiable return, gilts are not risk free. Once they have been issued, prices go up and down on the stock market. The key factors which make gilt prices move are the level of interest rates and the rate of inflation. Timing and anticipation are important when investing in gilts. Broadly, prices rise when interest rates fall, and fall when interest rates rise.

Investors can use gilts in two main ways:

- To secure a fixed return on their money over a number of years.

- To make a capital gain by buying gilts when prices are low and selling when they rise.

Before we look at how gilts may fit into your own investment plans it is important to understand the mechanics – and the jargon – of the gilts market.

Gilt prices are shown in the daily financial section of many newspapers. In the *Financial Times*, they are listed as British funds. The daily listings provide you with crucial information. As you will see from our illustration on p.81, each gilt has a coupon – the rate of interest paid on each £100 nominal stock issued and a redemption date – when that £100 will be paid back.

Confusingly, the coupon is not the real guide to the actual return investors get from a gilt – that depends on the price you pay for it. The price you will see in the daily list is what you pay for £100 nominal of gilt stock on the stock market. So to find out what your return would be at the current price,

UK GILTS - cash market

Mar 16	Notes	Price £	W'k % +/–	Amnt £m	Interest due	Last xd	City line
Shorts" (Lives up to Five Years)							
Tr Fltg Rate '01		100.04	....	3,000	8OcJaApJy	1.1	–
Cn 9½pc '01	✠	101.31	....	3	Ja12 Jy12	3.1	–
Cn 9¾pc '01	✠	101.74	....	35	Fe10 Au10	1.1	2201
Tr 2½pc IL '01		215.59xd	0.1	2,150	Mr24 Se24	15.3	1316
Tr 7pc '01		101.19	0.1	12,750	My6 Nv6	23.2	3031
Cn 10pc '02	✠	105.17	0.1	21	Oc11 Mr31	2.10	–
Tr 7pc '02		102.42	0.2	9,000	De7 Je7	28.11	–
Cn 9½pc '02	✠	105.40	0.2	2	De14 Je14	5.12	–
Tr 9¾pc '02		106.62	0.2	6,527	Fe27 Au27	16.2	1349
Tr 8pc '02–6		104.48	0.2	2,050	Ap5 Oc5	26.9	1334
Ex 9pc '02	✠	106.41	0.2	83	My19 Nv19	9.11	–
Tr 11¾pc '03–7	✠	111.86	0.2	234	Jy22 Ja22	11.1	1293
Cn 9¾pc '03	✠	109.63	0.3	11	Nv7 My7	27.10	–
Tr 8pc '03		106.43	0.3	6,999	Je10 De10	4.12	2010
Tr 10pc '03		111.71	0.3	1,768	Mr8 Se8	28.2	1281
Tr 12½pc '03–5	✠	118.80	0.3	152	My21 Nv21	10.11	1295
Tr 6½pc '03		104.09	0.5	7,987	Je7 De7	28.11	1800
Tr 13½pc '04–8	✠	124.09xd	0.4	95	Se26 Mr26	15.3	1301
Tr 10pc '04	✠	114.76	0.5	20	Nv18 My18	13.11	–
Tr 5pc '04		100.45	0.6	7,408	Je7 De7	28.11	–
Fnd 3½pc '99–4		96.15	0.4	543	Ja14 Jy14	4.1	1274
Cn 9½pc '04	✠	115.13	0.6	307	Ap25 Oc25	16.10	1246
Tr 6¾pc '04		106.47xd	0.6	6,500	My26 Nv26	15.3	3541
Cn 9½pc '05		116.92	0.6	4,804	Oc18 Ap18	9.10	1247
Five to Ten Years							
Ex 10½pc '05	✠	122.49xd	0.7	23	Mr20 Se20	9.3	–
Tr 8½pc '05		115.37	0.7	10,373	Je7 De7	28.11	4946
Tr 7¾pc '06		113.87	0.9	3,870	Mr8 Se8	28.2	2300
Cn 9¾pc '06	✠	124.20	0.9	6	My15 Nv15	6.11	–
Tr 7½pc '06		113.39	0.9	11,700	Je7 De7	28.11	1148

	Notes	Price £	W'k % +/–	Amnt £m	Interest due	Last xd	City line
Tr 8½pc '07		119.88	1.0	6,933	Ja16 Jy16	5.1	1339
Tr 7¼pc '07		114.08	1.1	11,000	Je7 De7	28.11	2504
Tr 5½pc '08–12		104.98	1.2	1,000	Mr10 Se10	1.3	1330
Tr 9pc '08		126.82	1.1	5,441	Ap13 Oc13	4.10	1343
Tr 8pc '09	✠	122.92xd	1.3	393	Mr25 Se25	15.3	1336
Tr 5¾pc '09		107.88	1.4	8,827	Je7 De7	28.11	–
Ten to Fifteen Years							
Tr 6¼pc '10		113.13	1.5	4,750	My25 Nv25	16.11	4632
Cn 9pc Ln '11		136.56	1.4	5,273	Jy12 Ja12	3.1	1245
Tr 7¾pc '12–15		125.30	1.5	800	Jy26 Ja26	17.1	1332
Tr 9pc '12		138.96	1.7	5,361	Fe6 Au6	26.1	1701
Tr 8pc '13		132.09xd	1.8	6,100	Mr27 Se27	16.3	2229
Tr 8pc '15		136.48	2.0	9,287	Je7 De7	4.12	4992
Over Fifteen Years							
Ex 12pc '13–17	✠	170.70	1.7	57	Je12 De12	4.12	1260
Tr 8¾pc '17		148.14	2.0	7,550	Fe25 Au25	15.2	1982
Tr 8pc '21		146.43	2.0	16,500	Je7 De7	28.11	2021
Tr 6pc '28		125.93	2.4	11,513	De7 Je7	28.11	2149
Tr 4¼pc '32		98.88	2.7	6,644	De7 Je7	28.11	–
Undated							
Cons 4pc	✠	83.62	3.6	358	Au1 Fe1	23.1	1239
War Ln 3½pc		76.08	3.3	1,909	Je1 De1	22.11	1352
Cn 3½pc '61 Aft.	✠	81.45	3.6	98	Ap1 Oc1	21.9	1243
Tr 3pc '66 Aft.	✠	58.43	3.4	55	Ap5 Oc5	26.9	1324
Cons 2½pc	✠	53.37	3.7	275	5JaApJyOc	27.12	1238
Tr 2½pc		52.76	3.2	474	Ap1 Oc1	21.9	1315

	Notes	Price £	W'k % +/–	Amnt £m	Interest due	Last xd
Index–Linked	**(b)**					
2½pc '03	(78.8)	212.61	0.3	2,700	My20 Nv20	9.11
4⅜pc '04	(135.6)	131.93	0.2	1,300	Ap21 Oc21	12.10
2pc '06	(69.5)	234.49	0.1	2,500	Ja19 Jy19	10.1
2½pc '09	(78.8)	218.03	0.2	2,625	My20 Nv20	9.11
2½pc '11	(74.6)	231.73	0.2	3,475	Fe23 Au23	14.2
2½pc '13	(89.2)	195.32	0.1	4,200	Fe16 Au16	7.2
2½pc '16	(81.6)	216.22	0.1	4,495	Ja26 Jy26	17.1
2½pc '20	(83.0)	217.32	....	4,175	Ap16 Oc16	5.10
2½pc '24	(97.7)	191.11	–.1	4,820	Ja17 Jy17	8.2
4⅛pc '30	(135.1)	188.85	–.4	2,150	Ja16 Jy22	11.1

(b) Figures in parentheses show RPI base for indexing, (months prior to issue) and have been adjusted to re rebasing of RPI to 100 in January 1987. Conversion fa 3.945. RPI for June 2000: 171.1 and for January 2001: 17

Other Fixed Interest

	Notes	Price £	W'k % +/–	Amnt £m	Interest due	Last xd
Asian Dev 10¼pc 2009		127	0.8	100	Mr24 Se24	20.3
B'ham 11½pc 2012		148	0.3	45	My15 Nv15	23.10
Leeds 13½pc 2006		136xd	0.7	40	Ap1 Oc1	14.3
Liverpool 3½pc Irred.		65xd	–1.5	5	1ApJyOcJa	7.3
LCC 3pc '20 Aft.		53	–3.6	26	1MrJeSeDe	21.2
Manchester 11½pc 2007		133	0.8	6	Ap25 Oc25	25.9
Met. Wtr. 3pc 'B'		93½	–.5	25	Mr1 Se1	21.2
N'wide Anglia 3⅞pc IL 2021		184	–.8	60	Ja30 Jy30	2.1
4¼pc IL 2024		176	–2.8	50	Au23 Fe23	29.1

● Source: Debt Management Office (DMO). All UK Gilts are tax-free to non-residents on application. xd Ex dividend. Closing mid-prices are shown in pounds per £100 nominal of stock. Weekly percentage changes are calculated a Friday to Friday basis. ✠ Indicative price. Gilts "runners", the benchmarks and most liquid stocks, are shown in bold type.

you must look further along the columns where you will see two kinds of yields.

- The interest yield tells you what return you get buying the gilt at the current market price. This is also known as the flat yield.

- The redemption yield tells you what you get when buying the gilt at the current market price and holding until it is repaid. The redemption yield takes into account the capital gains or losses made by investors on repayment, as well as the interest paid. It shows you the total return.

Two examples

Looking at our illustration on p. 81 you will see that Treasury 10 pc 2003 (Example A) is shown priced at £111.75 on the stock market. That is the price of £100 of nominal stock as all gilt prices are in pounds, not pence. The coupon is 10 per cent – that is the amount of interest you will receive on each £100 nominal of stock. But you are paying more than that nominal amount, so your actual return will be less – it will in fact work out at 8.95 per cent. That is the interest yield or flat yield.

The stock for which you have paid £111.75 will be repaid at its nominal value of £100 in the year 2000, so you will have a capital loss of just over £11.75 if you hold it until then. If you take that loss into account, your rate of return is reduced to 6.97 per cent if you hold it until repayment. That is the redemption yield.

Treasury 13 pc 2000 is what is known as a high-coupon gilt. The return is in the form of annual interest. As you look at the list, you may wonder why anyone would want to buy a low-coupon gilt – like Treasury 7 pc 2002 (Example B) for instance. But in the case of low-coupon gilts, the investment attraction is that what you may lose in interest, you make up as an assured return in the form of capital gain.

This gilt is priced at £101.93 – only just over the nominal value. It will be repaid at £100 in 2002 at the latest. So while the interest yield is 6.87 the redemption yield is higher than the 10 pc 2003 at 5.91, reflecting this capital gain. Since capital gains on gilts are tax exempt, low-coupon gilts are particularly attractive to higher-rate taxpayers.

Interest rates are actually calculated day by day. The daily financial press does the important sums for you and provides the information you need. You have to understand what the figures mean and also the characteristics of the main categories of gilts you will see listed.

- SHORT-DATED gilts are those with less than five years to redemption.

- MEDIUM-DATED gilts are those with redemption dates of between five and fifteen years.

- LONG-DATED gilts are those with over 15 years to redemption.

- UNDATED gilts have no set repayment date, and in practice are unlikely ever to be repaid. Take specialist advice before thinking of buying them.

- INDEX-LINKED gilts were introduced in the early 1980s when inflation was a major headache. Both the interest paid and the capital repayment are linked to the Retail Price Index which provides investors with a degree of certainty and security if they hold to redemption.

Take the 2½ pc 09 index linked stock shown. 2½ pc is the coupon – the amount paid for every £100 of nominal stock. That interest payment increases every six months in line with the official rate of inflation. The value of the £100 nominal stock, due for repayment in 2009 is also adjusted in line with the RPI, giving it a current indexed value. The actual market price at which the stock is bought or sold will be at a discount or a premium to this indexed value. The actual redemption value – what the stock will be worth when it is paid back – is unknown and depends on the rate of inflation between now and then. So market prices for index-linked gilts are governed by expectations of inflation.

These index-linked gilts, it is fair to say, have been of more interest to pension funds than individual investors but financial advisers sometimes recommend a holding to higher rate taxpayers to protect their capital from inflation.

The length of time to repayment is an important factor in gilt prices. 'Shorts' for instance are more sensitive to the current level of interest rates. Investors may compare the return on the short-dated gilt with what they might get from a building society or some other income-generating investment that matures within a few years.

'Longs' and 'mediums' are more difficult to judge since they require a degree of crystal-ball gazing. While they offer the investor an assured fixed income for a number of years, you have to think carefully about the future level of both interest rates and inflation – particularly if you intend holding until redemption.

Usually you will find that the longer-dated gilts offer highest yields – reflecting the normal investment rule that the longer you 'tie up' your money, the higher the return. But you can get an 'inverse' yield curve where 'shorts' are showing higher yields. This indicates that interest rates are expected to fall – the lower yields on 'longs' reflect what the stock market thinks will happen in the future.

High inflation is not good news for conventional gilts, nor any fixed-income investment, because it eats into the real value of the income – and the real value of the capital at redemption. High inflation inevitably means that gilt prices fall since yields must rise to compensate for the reduction in real returns.

Timing is also important when it comes to interest rates. If you go into gilts when interest rates are low, you stand to lose out when they rise because your return is 'fixed' when you buy – so you are missing out on a better deal – and the market price for gilts will go down as interest rates rise. When you consider the ups and downs in interest rates over the past few years you will see why gilts can be a very volatile investment despite their safe image.

The best time to buy gilts is when interest rates are high – and expected to fall. That way you secure a high fixed return (either in the form of income or capital) and have the option of taking a capital gain by selling your stock when interest rates fall and the market price rises.

Most investors who buy gilts are less interested in 'playing the market' by buying and selling gilts than in having a proportion of their portfolio with a guaranteed return on a medium to long-term basis.

Choosing gilts

Which gilts you buy depends on your investment objectives – and your tax situation. Investors wanting high income should look for a high coupon gilt with a good interest yield and a redemption date that reflects the length of time you plan to invest for. If you retire at 60, for instance, and need a good income from your investments over the next 15 to 20 years you will find an appropriately dated gilt among the 'longs' listed. There will be a capital loss if you hold to redemption – but that may be acceptable if your priority is maximizing the ongoing income from your investments. There may be less point in the high-income seeker buying short-dated gilts – even if the yield happens to be higher. But there can be no absolute rule. This is a complex subject, where timing is crucial, and many investors prefer to take expert advice.

For investors paying higher-rate tax who do not need an immediate high income, low-coupon gilts are more attractive since most of the return will be in the form of a capital gain when the nominal amount is paid back rather than the annual interest. Capital gains on gilts are tax-exempt and low coupon gilts can be a useful part of a growth portfolio.

While undated gilts are best left to the experts, carefully chosen index-linked gilts guarantee investors a 'real' return over and above the rate of inflation. Both the capital repayment and interest payments are linked to the movement of the Retail Price Index, so they offer the certainty of beating inflation. It is fair to say that index-linked gilts have not proved so popular in recent years when inflation has been seen to be under control.

Buying gilts

You can buy gilts through a stockbroker, financial adviser or a bank where similar commission charges will apply as with all other investments. It is also possible for individual investors to buy gilts through the Bank of England, where an 'execution only' postal service is available and the rate of commission is normally lower than through a stockbroker, particularly for smaller transactions. A free booklet is available entitled 'Investing in gilts – the private investor's guide to investing in British Government Stocks' giving details on how to buy and sell gilts from the Bank of England.*

---

*See **Chapter 16, Useful Addresses**, pp. 141–2, for details of how to order this booklet.

10

Tax-Free Investments

Over the past few years governments have been keen to stimu-late personal savings. The result has been the introduction of tax concessions for certain kinds of investments. The prin-ciple behind this is that savers can invest up to a maximum sum and pay no tax on the proceeds.

Personal Equity Plans (PEPs) and Tax Exempt Special Savings Accounts (TESSAs) were the first of these types of investments and proved hugely popular with the investing public. Labour replaced these vehicles with a new financial vehicle designed to extend the principle of tax concessions for long-term savings and investment, the ISA. The ISA is designed to make investing for the future a much easier and attainable option for everyone. ISAs allow you to save in cash, life insurance and stocks and shares, and are available to any UK resident over 18 years old. However, from 1 April 2001, 16 and 17 year olds can invest in a cash ISA.

There are two different types of ISA; the maxi and mini. You are allowed to open only one maxi ISA, or up to three different mini ISAs in any one tax year.

The maxi ISA

The maxi ISA allows you to invest in cash, stocks and shares and life insurance under one account, with one ISA manager looking after all your savings. You can invest up to £7,000 in a maxi; this can be up to £3,000 in cash, up to £1,000 in insurance, and up to £5,000 in stocks and shares. However, should you decide not to invest in cash or insurance, you can invest the full £7,000 in stocks and shares. These limits have recently been extended until April 2006.

The mini ISA

There are three mini ISAs – one each for cash, stocks and shares, and life insurance. The Inland Revenue suggests that this may benefit those who want a separate fund manager for each element of their savings, although it will be possible to hold all types of mini ISA with the same manager. You can invest up to £3,000 in a cash mini ISA, £1,000 in an insurance mini ISA and £3,000 in a stocks and shares mini ISA.

After 5 April 2001, the allowances for ISAs will decrease so that the maximum investment will be £5,000. With the maxi ISA this can be made up of £5,000 worth of stocks, or a proportion of this £5,000 can be allocated to cash (£1,000 maximum) or insurance (again £1,000 maximum). The allowances for cash mini ISAs will be £1,000, insurance mini ISAs £1,000 and stocks and shares mini ISAs up to £3,000.

The cash element of ISAs can include savings accounts and National Savings products. Stocks and shares can include unit trusts, investment trusts, OEICS, corporate bonds, and UK government gilts with at least five years to maturity. Not all life insurance policies can be included within your ISA. Your

ISA manager may be able to provide you with a range of policies, or a list of acceptable policies from different issuers.

Tax benefits

All interest, dividends and bonuses from cash, and stocks and shares held in an ISA are exempt from income tax, and none of your savings need to be reported on your tax returns. Capital gains on ISA investments are also exempt from Capital Gains Tax, though any losses incurred from ISA investments cannot be allowed for CGT purposes against capital gains elsewhere. Dividend payments on shares in UK-based companies will carry a 10 per cent tax credit, and this will be refunded through your ISA account manager. However, this 10 per cent tax credit is to be completely abolished in April 2004.

How should I choose an ISA?

There is a vast array of ISAs available from High Street banks and building societies, fund managers and other investment organizations. When opening an ISA think carefully about the following points:

- Make sure you are aware of all the terms and conditions and fees you might incur in running your ISA. This may include general management fees, transaction charges or fees for withdrawing funds.

- Decide how much you want to save. Bear in mind that this can be in monthly instalments, or a one-off payment.

- Consider how quickly you might want access to your savings. Some ISAs will pay better rates of interest if you agree to a specific notice period before withdrawing from the account, ranging from a few days to several months; think about this carefully before tying up your money.

- Consider what level of risk you are prepared to take, particularly in relation to stocks and shares and unit-linked life policies.

- Decide which ISA most closely suits your needs and then shop around for the best deal. Remember to consider the whole tax year – are you likely to receive a lump sum later in the year, perhaps from a maturing Employee Share Scheme? If so, take care over opening a cash ISA since this would limit the amount of shares you can hold in an ISA to just £3,000.

Other things to bear in mind when choosing your ISA are whether you are looking for income or growth. Like unit and investment trusts, different plans have different investment objectives. If you wish to have individual shares in your ISA, you will need to choose the self-select variety. Some ISA managers allow monthly contributions into an ISA instead of a lump sum investment.

With a 'managed' ISA, you should look for one with a good track record. Investment performance is more important than the level of charges in the long term. But remember that past performance is not necessarily a guide to future returns.

With a 'self-select' ISA, you want one that allows you to switch investments cheaply and easily. These are offered by many stockbrokers.

You should look for an ISA that complements your

existing investments. If you already have unit trusts, for instance, you might use your ISA to invest in individual shares. If you have a portfolio of shares, you might want a unit or investment trust ISA instead.

CAT Standards

Some ISAs conform to CAT Standards, standing for fair Charges, easy Access and decent Terms. These have been introduced by the government to help new investors decide upon which ISA provider to use. Their use is purely voluntary but they indicate a variety of user friendly features incorporating minimum charges for transactions and investment management, and easy and quick access to savings. However, CAT Standards should not be regarded as an indication of good investment prospects, they only relate to the conditions attached to the ISA.

Employee Share Ownership

Should you be receiving shares from either a Sharesave or a Profit Sharing Scheme you can transfer these directly into the stocks and shares component of your ISA within a period of 90 days from the date they emerge from the scheme.

PEPs and TESSAs

PEPs and TESSAs have been replaced by ISAs. However, you do not have to sell your PEPs, or transfer your TESSA investments into an ISA. From 6 April 1999, you were no longer able to contribute to your PEP investments though you can still contribute to your TESSA up to the annual limit, their tax breaks will remain the same, and you will still be able to transfer between TESSA and PEP providers/managers.

There is also a TESSA-only ISA in which you can transfer your TESSA investments on maturity (restricted to the capital invested) up to £9,000, without affecting your yearly ISA investment level.

National Savings

National Savings has a variety of investment products, some of which offer tax-free returns. You can get details and application forms from the Post Office.

Fixed Interest Savings Certificates

You can invest a lump sum of between £100 and £10,000 for a guaranteed tax-free return after five years in each issue. Your capital is secure and you can cash in your certificates at any time but you should hold them for the full five years to get the maximum return as the interest rate increases each year to maturity. When you compare returns on National Savings Certificates with what is available from banks and building societies remember that the latter usually quote a gross return upon which you will have to pay tax. A higher rate taxpayer, for instance, would need a return of 10 per cent gross on a deposit to equal a tax-free return of 6 per cent.

Index-Linked Savings Certificates

These are similar to FISCs but the return is based on the rise in the Retail Price Index over the five years to maturity plus an increasing amount of extra interest each year. Interesting if you think inflation is going to start rising and a simpler cheaper alternative to investing in index-linked gilts.

Insurance Linked Savings Schemes

These schemes produce tax-free returns for savers prepared to tuck their money away on a regular basis over the long term. The best known schemes are the with-profits endowment policies taken out to fund mortgages. But many other savers, attracted by a tax-free return if the plan runs for the statutory ten years, find them a good way to build up a lump sum. Money is invested in the insurance company's own internal fund and annual bonuses are added to your savings depending on how smart the fund management has been. Before choosing a policy, look at both the past investment record of the managers and the level of charges, which can eat up a lot of the investment value in the early years.

11

Personal Pensions

It cannot be said too often: a pension is one of the most important aspects of your financial planning. Like your mortgage, your insurance and your 'rainy day' cash, making sure that you will have enough money in retirement must be a top priority – it is a cornerstone of your overall savings strategy. Even if you are already contributing to an employer's pension scheme, and are happy to stay there, you should look carefully to see if you should be making 'top ups' through a personal pension plan.

Both the present and the previous government have been keen to promote the savings habit. When it comes to personal pensions the tax incentives are very generous indeed. Not surprisingly this has spawned a huge pensions industry with plenty of salespeople enticing you to buy this or that plan. It can all be very confusing and independent advice is often hard to come by. There are, however, a few general points to consider when planning your pension.

Start early if you want to make sure of building up a decent pension to retire on. Each year you delay means that it will cost you more to create the same amount of pension at the end of your working life. The sooner you invest the money, the more opportunity there is for your pension savings to grow over the years.

Inflation may be low now but it is still a vital factor in assessing the real value of your future pension. Basic living costs will rise by the time you come to retire. What will that do to the spending power of what you are expecting to receive when you stop earning? Your dependants will need to be looked after financially whether you die before or after retirement. Whatever pension scheme you choose, you must look carefully at these arrangements as well.

Everyone is now entitled to have a personal pension plan – even if they work for an employer that offers a pension scheme. One of the most difficult decisions is whether to join a company scheme, or to opt for the personal pension plans sold by a large number of insurance companies, investment houses, banks and other financial institutions. It is important to understand the basic differences between the two.

Company pensions

Company pensions may offer a pension based on the amount of your salary when you retire. These are known as 'final salary' pension schemes. Both you and the employer will contribute a percentage of your earnings to the fund. There will be a range of other benefits too – a widow's or widower's pension, for instance, and life insurance offering payment to dependants if you die before retirement. The most attractive part of a final salary scheme is that there is the prospect of an increase in the value of your pension once it is being paid. These are the plus points.

The main disadvantage is when you change jobs; the structure of company pension schemes favours those who remain in the same employment for a long time. Even though you can now take the 'transfer value' of your pension to a new employer you may still lose out. Frequent job changes mean that you can end up with bits of pension from a number of past employers. An increasing number of companies are now switching from final salary to what are known as 'money purchase' schemes. In these, the amount of your pension is not linked to salary but to the return on the 'pension pot' you have built up.

On the other hand, a company pension scheme, particularly a final salary scheme, is usually very good value for older employees who don't expect to move jobs before retirement. No one should opt out of an employer's scheme without taking independent advice. Most people are better off staying put. One of the disastrous results of the liberalization of pension regulations was that many people were tempted out of final salary company pension schemes, only to discover that the personal pensions they had bought did not match up in terms of the eventual benefits.

Personal pensions

Personal pensions are best for the young who expect to change jobs several times during their working lives and they are essential if there is no employer's scheme on offer with your job or if you are self-employed. It is vital to understand the difference between a personal pension and an employer's scheme. A personal pension means that you have your own individual 'pot' of money that you can contribute to as and how you like, regardless of who you are working for. The main disadvantage is that the employer does not contribute to the pension (though there is nothing to stop them doing so if you can negotiate it) and there is no guaranteed level of pension. What you get depends on the amount of pension, in the form of an annuity, that your 'pension pot' can buy you when you retire, rather than on the amount of your salary. This is a very important distinction.

An annuity is a regular income that you buy from an insurance company when you retire using the money invested in your personal pension plan. You can buy your annuity between your 50th and 70th birthday.

Choosing a personal pension

There is a baffling range of personal pension plans on the market and since the size of your pension depends on the amount of money you can build up, it is important to choose carefully. The first thing to consider is how you want your pension money, or premiums, invested.

Unit-linked pension plan

Unit-linked pension plans give you a choice of different kinds of funds managed by the insurance or investment company. Typically there will be a wide range of equity funds where money is invested on the stock market, including overseas shares. There will probably be a Far East or North American fund into which you can put your money. There is also likely to be a property fund, a fixed-interest and cash fund and a managed fund that invests across the whole range, which is useful if you want to spread your risk. You may also be offered a 'tracker' or index fund which aims to match a specific stock market index – the FTSE 100 for instance.

Clearly, you want to look hard at the investment performance of these funds, bearing in mind that short-term ups and downs may not mean very much when you are tucking away money for the long haul. The further it is until your retirement date, the more risk you may be prepared to take, investing in equity funds for instance, but the nearer you get to retirement the more predictability you need. This is the time to secure your stock market gains, for example by putting your money in the cash fund. You can switch your money between different funds. If you go the unit-linked route you will need all your investment knowledge to make the most of your money.

With-profits pension plan

With-profits pension plans invest the premiums in the insurance or investment company's own fund, which will be a mixture of shares, gilts and maybe property. You will be guaranteed a minimum amount each year plus a share of the profits of the investment fund. The crucial difference between this and a unit-linked pension plan is that these profits, once given, cannot be taken away – and you should get a final bonus added to your fund when you retire. Again it is important to look at the bonus record of the pension provider as this will be a guide, though it is no cast-iron guarantee of what will happen in the future.

The ideal way to invest your pension money is often to use both types of plan, the unit-linked to give you the opportunity for capital appreciation in the stock market and the with-profits to provide a more secure, predictable investment. It is always sensible to spread the risks when you invest and this principle applies equally to your pension plan.

There is nothing to stop you taking out more than one pension plan though you should enquire about the level of charges, which can vary enormously, but bear in mind that in the long run, investment performance will be more important. As a personal discipline, a regular-premium policy where you make contributions each month or year is a good idea, but you can make a series of one-off payments through single-premium plans instead or use them to top up your pension payments as and when you can afford it.

How much to invest?

Sellers of pension plans will present you with a battery of figures about how much pension your contributions will buy you in 20 or 30 years' time. You should understand that these are only estimates, based on assumptions about investment performance. They are not promises or guarantees. You also have to think about the impact of inflation on the often rather attractive amounts of pension that are illustrated. The important point to remember is that the sooner you invest, the more chance your pension savings have to increase in value. Even if you can make only modest contributions initially you can increase these later on as you earn more money and have fewer financial responsibilities.

Tax

One of the most attractive features of saving through a pension scheme is the generous tax concessions. You can get full tax relief on your pension contributions up to a maximum proportion of your earnings. And under present Inland Revenue rules the older you are the higher the proportion of your income you can pay in. You can get full tax relief on up to 17½ per cent of your taxable earnings if you are 35 or younger – but this proportion rises in stages according to your age. At age 51, for instance, your limit will be 30 per cent. So you should check what your limit is with the tax man.

If you are employed you will make contributions to your personal pension plan net of basic-rate tax and claim any higher-rate tax relief from the tax man. If you are self-employed you will make your contributions gross and claim the tax back on your tax return form.

If you don't invest up to the maximum in the tax year – and few of us do – you can make it up later on when you have more money. You can go back six years and utilize any unused tax allowances as well as getting your maximum tax relief for the current year.

Additional voluntary contributions (AVCs)

If you are in an employer's scheme but want to put more money into your pension, you can do so through an AVC. First you have to look at what percentage of your earnings you are already contributing. You can get full tax relief on extra contributions, provided the total that you contribute is not more than 15 per cent of your earnings. Many employers offer an AVC scheme of their own, but you are perfectly entitled to buy an independent one from any insurance or investment company of your choice. If you opt for an employer's AVC there should be no charges, but you should enquire carefully about the terms and ask exactly what your extra contributions are buying you. If you buy a free-standing AVC from an insurance company you will pay commission, which may be worth it if the benefits look better. Compare deals to find out what is best.

The tax concession on pension contributions, whether you are taking out a personal pension plan or topping up with an AVC, make them very attractive ways of saving money. But while you should make sure you are building up a decent pension, it is a mistake to make this your only form of saving. Pensions are inflexible compared with other kinds of investments. Although you can take some of your money in a lump sum, the rest has to be paid as pension. What you get in the end depends on how long you, or your dependants, live.

It is not the same as having, for instance, a portfolio of shares or unit trusts that you can cash in when you want to. For this reason many investors prefer to have an ISA plan, for instance, rather than an AVC. It is important to strike a balance.

SIPPS

It is possible to run your own pension through a self-invested personal pension plan. The benefit of SIPPS is that you have complete control over your own pension and can make your own investment decisions related to it. There are a wide variety of investments which can be held in a SIPP – equities and bonds traded on any recognized stock exchange in the world, unit and investment trusts, insurance company funds, deposit accounts and commercial property. If you are self-employed, you can even invest in your own business.

SIPPS enable those people that have the time and experience to choose a portfolio of individual company shares to manage their own pension. The advantage over a normal pension scheme is that because the fund management and administration roles are completely separate, you can change fund managers more easily and do not have to swap your whole plan, which can be time consuming and costly. The costs involved will be two-fold. First there is the cost of administrating the scheme, plus the normal charges associated with trading shares. For this reason, SIPPS are not really suitable unless you have a substantial sum to invest – over £100,000 as a broad guideline. Those who have less knowledge, time or money to invest, would be best advised to steer clear and leave this to the experts. It is not wise to play with your retirement income unless you really know what you are doing and understand the implications.

Stakeholder pensions

The government has announced that individual pension accounts (or stakeholder pensions) will be available from April 2001. These low-cost, flexible personal pensions will have transparent charges of 1 per cent per annum or less and will be accessible through insurers, banks and even supermarkets. It will make buying a pension much more like buying a unit trust or investment trust direct from a fund manager, rather than buying a complicated contract from the life assurance companies that currently dominate the pensions market.

As with ordinary personal pensions, the levels of contribution will vary according to age, but for the first time people not in paid employment will be able to contribute – up to £3,600 a year. Tax relief will apply at the highest rate on contributions to encourage people to make provision for their retirement.

12

Tax

Tax can be a complex subject. The application and impact of tax laws can vary widely from case to case. For this reason this book can only provide general guidance and if you are concerned about your tax position you should consult a professional adviser such as a chartered accountant. The Inland Revenue also produce a range of easy to understand booklets which are available free of charge at www.inlandrevenue.gov or from your local tax office.

Never invest in something just because of a tax break. This does not mean that you should ignore the tax factor when it comes to your investment strategy. As an investor you can be taxed in two ways: on income from shares and in tax payable on the growth in the value of your investments when you come to sell them. It is vital to know the basic rules and how you can, quite legally, reduce your tax bill by organizing your investments in the most efficient way. If you have your own business, or a large investment portfolio, you may have access to professional tax advice, but all investors should have a working knowledge of the way taxation policies affect them, particularly as the Self Assessment system puts more responsibility on taxpayers themselves. There are important differences in the tax treatment of the various investment products too.

Tax free investments

'Tax free' investment means just that – you are not liable for tax on your investment returns. Examples include many of the National Savings products and ISAs offered by most financial institutions. Provided you stick to the rules, all returns – whether in the form of income or capital – are tax free to the investor. The Individual Savings Account which the government introduced in 1999 extends the long-held principle that people can be encouraged to save by offering them tax free returns. Tax free investments, however, don't offer any tax concessions on the money you put into savings. At the moment you can only get tax relief on money you put into a pension plan.

Some investments pay income gross to investors without the deduction of tax. Examples include the National Savings Investment Account, all gilts and income from offshore deposits. This does not mean that you are not liable for tax on this investment income – you are, unless your total income is so low that you don't pay tax at all. This subject has been dealt with in some detail in Chapter 10 (pp. 88–94).

Stamp Duty

Stamp duty is a tax on buying shares that you have to pay to the government. New rules brought in from October 1999 set stamp duty at 0.5 per cent of the value of the share purchase, with a minimum charge of £5. For all charges above this minimum, the rate of stamp duty will be rounded up to the nearest £5. For any transactions involving unit trusts the original levy of £0.50 in every £100 still applies (£0.50 minimum charge). Your stockbroker will add this tax to the cost of any shares that you buy. When share purchases are settled electronically within CREST the transaction is liable to Stamp Duty Reserve Tax (SDRT). This is charged at an exact rate of 0.5 per cent (with no rounding up) of the initial purchase price.

Tax on income from investment

When you receive dividend payments from the companies you are invested in, normally twice a year, these will be paid with 10 per cent tax deducted. If you do not pay tax, you will not be able to reclaim this credit. Basic rate taxpayers will have no more income tax to pay. For those who pay tax at the higher rate, a special rate of 32.5 per cent will be applied to their dividend income and they will have to pay the extra 22.5 per cent (over the 10% tax credit) to the Inland Revenue at the end of the tax year.

Married couples may be able to reduce their total income tax bills by organizing their investments in a tax-efficient way. The current system of independent taxation means that both partners can claim personal tax allowances. If one partner is not earning or paying basic rate tax and the other is paying higher rate tax, it would make sense to transfer income-producing investments into their name. This will save the additional 22.5 per cent tax being paid by the higher-rate tax payer on any dividends received.

Tax on growth in value of investments (CGT)

Capital Gains Tax (CGT) is payable on the increase in the capital value of your investments when you sell them. Shares are the obvious example. In the case of building society 'windfall' shares, the purchase price will be taken as nil. The rate of CGT you pay depends on your own top rate of income tax, but a generous annual exemption, currently £7,200, means that many individual investors should pay little or no CGT.

It is very important that you keep up-to-date records of all your investments – the prices at which you buy and sell shares and the income you receive from them. If you do that it should not be too difficult to work out how much, if anything, you owe the tax man. Here are some important points to note when calculating CGT:

- You can make profits of up to £7,200 during the tax year without paying any CGT at all.

- You can offset any losses against your capital gains in the same tax year. For instance if you have sold shares at £8,000 profit but have taken a loss of £3,000 your overall profit will be reduced to £5,000 – well below the level of the CGT exemption.

- You can offset capital losses against gains in future tax years.

- You can only use the CGT exemption for that current tax year – you can't carry it forward to use in future years.

The rate of CGT payable by an individual will be 10 per cent, 20 per cent or 40 per cent, depending upon the level of tax paid by the individual. When calculating whether any CGT is payable, you are able to deduct any costs of buying or selling the shares (e.g. stamp duty on purchase and broker's commission on both purchase and sale) from the gain you have made.

For shares bought before 5 April 1998 and sold at profit subsequently, you can also add to your purchase price (including acquisition costs) any percentage increase in the general level of retail prices from when you bought the shares up until that date. You cannot, however, add the indexation factor if you have made a loss on the shares. The Inland Revenue publishes a table showing (if you have sold shares in that month) the indexation factor that can be added to the purchase price of your shares in arriving at your CGT calculation. The situation changed with effect from 6 April 1998 when the government announced that indexation would be replaced by the tapering of capital gains. The taper reduces the amount of the taxable gain according to how long the asset has been held since 5 April 1998 as follows:

Gains on non-business assets

Number of complete years after 5.4.98 for which asset held	Percentage of gain chargeable	Equivalent tax rates for higher/basic rate taxpayer
0	100	40/20
1	100	40/20
2	100	40/20
3	95	38/19
4	90	36/18
5	85	34/17
6	80	32/16
7	75	30/15
8	70	28/14
9	65	26/13
10 or more	60	24/12

If you bought shares before 5 April 1998 and sold them after this date then you will have to calculate your CGT liability in two stages. Indexation should be applied for the period from when the shares were bought until 5 April 1998 to increase the cost of your initial investment in line with inflation. But for the period from 6 April 1998 until the date on which the shares are sold (and the gain is realized) the tapering system described above should be used. Assets acquired before 17 March 1998 will be given one bonus year of taper relief. For shares bought after 1 April 1998 no indexation allowance can be used in calculating the CGT liability.

How to make the best use of the ground rules

Following these ground rules provides scope for reducing your tax bill with some easy planning. Married couples should divide their investments to take full advantage of their individual CGT exemptions. Your portfolio should be reviewed carefully towards the end of each tax year in order to use the annual CGT exemption. If you have built up large profits in one share you might want to take them or offset them with some of your losses.

For further information on indexation and the tapering system, ProShare produces the Portfolio Management System. This simple but effective paper-based system will enable you to keep track of your portfolio and account to the Inland Revenue. For further details see Chapter 15.

13

New Issues, Take-over Bids, Rights and Scrip Issues

Many people became shareholders for the first time when they bought shares in British Telecom, British Gas and other major privatizations. Millions more became shareholders when their building societies turned themselves into banks and floated their shares on the stock market. The privatizations and the building society flotations were both new issues, but bigger and more spectacular examples of how companies come to the stock market.

Going back to the basis of a stock market, selling shares in a company is the alternative to borrowing money from the bank to finance expansion. Offering shares in your company to the public encapsulates the original capital-raising function of a stock market. For investors it is an opportunity to buy shares without paying commission and to get them at an attractive price.

Unfortunately many companies now make their stock market debut through what is known as a 'placing'. Shares are sold to financial institutions and it is difficult for individual shareholders to get a look in unless they approach the stockbroker that is helping to organize the flotation. The placing is a cheaper and more convenient way for companies to go to the stock market.

A company may choose to make shares available to the public at a fixed price through newspaper advertisements. You can apply for the prospectus, which gives you details and the prospects for the company. This is known as a 'public offer' or 'offer for sale'. Traditionally, prospectuses have been paper reports, but now more of these are on-line or e-mailed by companies to prospective investors.

Increasingly, companies will make their shares available to a section of the public, usually existing customers. This has been a popular method, particularly so amongst Internet start-ups.

Assessing new issues

If you do spot a public offer you like the look of, the safest way of assessing whether it is a good buy is probably press comment. Newspapers do get it wrong sometimes, but they usually have a good idea whether the company is a goer or a flop. Lots of good publicity usually ensures a successful flotation, but not always. Lastminute.com is a famous example of a much publicized share that fell below its issue price soon after flotation. Companies and their advisers want to be sure that there will be plenty of takers for the shares, so they try and price them at a level that will show a nice little profit on the first day of dealings. This profit is known as a premium.

On the downside, the shares will have no track record and be a bit of an unknown quantity, making them more risky than investments in more established companies. For this reason it is important to look carefully at the prospectus. Compare the p/e ratio and dividend yield of the company with other companies in the same line of business. A new issue will often be valued a little lower than its established rivals. Judge each new issue on its own merits and buy because you believe in the company and what is says it will achieve. You should look at the lead broker or adviser and see whether they are well known and whether they have a good track record of bringing new companies to the market.

If you would like to apply to receive shares once you have read the prospectus, then you will need to register your interest. Again, traditionally this has been done by post or telephone, but it is now in many instances possible by e-mail. You should register your interest at an early stage as it creates no obligation to apply and some new issues move forward very quickly, so it is easy to miss the boat. A flotation where the administration for the whole process is handled on-line is known as an EPO (Electronic Public Offering). Once a company makes a formal announcement that it intends to float, it will give a price range in which it thinks the launch price will be – although this will be likely to change according to demand.

If a new issue is very popular it may be oversubscribed, meaning there are more applications for shares than there are shares on offer. You will probably have heard about people applying for shares in lastminute.com being peeved because they only received a very small parcel of shares compared to the quantity they applied for. This is because people wanted more shares than were available. This is quite common and there are various solutions, ranging from letting everyone who wants shares have them – but not as many as they want as with lastminute.com – to only letting a limited number of people have all of the shares they want whilst everyone else loses out. If the offer is oversubscribed, the offer price may be increased so that you have to reconfirm your interest at the higher price.

Of course things can go wrong with a first-time flotation even if the company looks solid enough. Sudden bad economic news can depress the stock market in the vital days between the announcement of an offer and the time dealings actually start. In that case the shares may fall below the offer price, going to what is known as a discount. Surplus shares are taken up by City institutions that have agreed to underwrite the new issue (an insurance against things going wrong) and it can take shares a long time to recover.

You will find out about larger new issues in the press – it would have been hard to miss the hype surrounding the issue of Thomson shares, Freeserve or lastminute.com. For less well known companies coming to market you will need to keep an eye on specialist investment publications – both *Shares* magazine and *Investors' Chronicle* have a new issues section providing information on those companies coming to the market, the final date for applications, the market it will be listed on – AIM, OFEX, main market, etc. – and the broker that is bringing the company to market.

Specialist services have developed to alert private investors to forthcoming new issues. One of the most comprehensive is DigitalLook.com which gives all the latest news, information and commentary on forthcoming stock market flotations. The service will include links to up-to-date news from media sources and the Internet, as well as the latest commentary from investors themselves, taken from the bulletin boards.

Other useful new issues services include www.issues direct.com, www.shareissues.com, www.newissues-ipo.com and hemscott.net's service www.hemscott.net. The London

Stock Exchange web site at www.londonstockexchange.com is also developing a service for private investors, which will provide a list of forthcoming new issues, including information about the company and its business together with details of the offer and the company's advisers.

Historically, due to the fact that many new issues trade at a premium to their issue price soon after launch, investors do get involved in new issues to make a quick buck and sell the investment on the first day of trading – a process known as 'stagging'. It is potentially possible to make a good return by stagging an investment, as it is by betting on a horse race, but there are many risks associated with this practice. If you are able to gain the allocation of shares that you want, you may not find it as easy to sell them again quickly enough to realize the gain. It is common for newly listed companies, particularly those that have been oversubscribed, to take a little while to send out share certificates. While some brokers will allow you to deal without a share certificate, others will insist that you have it first and you may find yourself unable to sell your shares to realize a gain or limit a loss soon after launch. Companies do not like this practice as the share price of a newly issued company can plummet as 'stags' offload their investments and send the share price down. Stagging is one of the reasons why the number of new issues available to the public has declined over recent years.

Take-over bid

When a company finds itself on the receiving end of a take-over bid, it can mean a nice bonus for shareholders.

To encourage them to accept the offer, the bidder will offer an amount in cash or shares, or a combination of the two, above the current stock market price. A hostile bid may prove a bonanza as the bidding company may have to increase its offer in the face of fierce resistance from the board or a counter bid from another predator.

Take-over activity tends to go in cycles – witness the explosion in activity in the 1980s when huge take-overs hit the headlines. When the stock market is going strong, companies on the prowl can use the enhanced value of their shares to make acquisitions. When the share prices are weak, take-overs become less popular.

Identifying bid targets

Investors can keep an eye out for likely bid targets to add a bit of speculative spice to their share portfolio. Read the financial press – there are often bid rumours reported which may be worth investigating, and look for other signs. These might include the acquisition of a large block of shares in a company by another group, which may herald the start of a take-over. Sometimes the stake is sold on, sometimes the purchaser just sits there with it, but sometimes a bid does materialize, though you can never bank on it.

Companies held back by uninspired management may be a bid target. If a company seems to be lagging behind its sector rivals, find out why. Another company may well see an opportunity to make more money out of a basically sound business that is poorly managed. Companies that are weighed down by loss-making divisions, heavy borrowings or over-expansion are vulnerable to a take-over. A predator may see a good financial opportunity in reorganizing the business by cutting losses and selling off the profitable parts.

When a take-over bid is announced, you do not have to do

anything immediately. If it is opposed by the existing board you will receive masses of information from both sides over the next few weeks. You can be fairly certain that the first offer made will be increased. Even if the bid is agreed by both sides, there is always the chance of a higher counter-offer from another company. Keep an eye on the market price of the shares. If it is higher than the value of the offer, it tells you that a better one is expected. Even if no rival bidder emerges, the predator often has to improve on the initial offer to secure acceptance from the big financial institutions. The only thing to watch out for at this stage is the possibility of the bid being referred to the Competition Commission which keeps an eye on take-overs and mergers. A reference usually kills the bid stone dead because it means months of investigation. If you think there is a strong chance of a referral you might want to sell your shares in the stock market while the going is good.

There are all kinds of City rules and regulations on take-overs, most of which need not concern shareholders. The official offer document you receive will set out the terms of the bid and the closing date for acceptance.

There is little point in accepting at once, although if you accept and the bidder is later forced to make a higher offer, you will get the higher offer in most circumstances, so you do not lose out. But while there is the chance of a rival bid there is nothing to be lost by waiting. At some point, however, you are going to have to make some decisions.

Decision time

Not all bids succeed. Some companies mount successful campaigns to keep their independence in the face of a take-over attempt, getting the backing of loyal shareholders. What you decide is up to you. You must look at the detail of the offer. It may be all cash or all shares or a combination of both. Often there is an offer of shares with a cash alternative. You have to choose.

The value of any share offer to you depends on the market price and prospects of the bidding company – often its share price falls a little during the course of a bid. You have to consider whether you want shares in that company. The advantage of taking a share offer is that you are not liable for Capital Gains Tax when you swap. This is important if you have built up a sizeable profit on your holding. If you take a cash offer you might be liable for CGT. Much depends on the amount of profit and the way you use your annual CGT exemption. On the other hand, cash means certainty – you know exactly how much you are going to get. But before you accept a cash offer you should compare it with the value of your shares on the stock market. If they are higher, sell there instead.

Rights issues

When a quoted company wants to raise money it can either borrow from the bank or asks its shareholders to put up the cash by buying more shares. The latter is obviously the cheapest option for the company. However, a rights issue, as it is called, is rarely popular with shareholders who regard it as an occupational hazard of stock market investment.

But it is not necessarily all bad news. Rights issues can result in a substantial fall in company borrowings and interest which benefits profits and earnings and can be a good way of financing expansion. Alternatively a rights issue may be a response to a crisis, launched as a last-ditch effort to save a company from going under. Whether you take up your rights to the shares or not may depend on what you feel about the company's prospects. You will be sent a document detailing the offer and telling you how the money will be used. You can find out what the market thinks about the rights issue by reading the press or asking your stockbroker.

You will be offered new shares in proportion to the amount you already have. So a rights issue may be one share for every three or four or five you hold. The price of the new shares will be below the current market price – 20 per cent is a rough average – to entice you to buy, but the announcement of rights issue will have an immediate effect on the value of your existing holding and the share price may initially fall in value – by how much depends on the size and the terms of the issue. The adjusted price is called the ex-rights price.

There is no reason why individual shareholders should buy new shares if they do not want to. If the company is basically sound, the financial institutions will have them. But you have to face the fact that, at least for the moment, the value of your holding may well be less and the company's earnings will be diluted. Alternatively, you may welcome an opportunity to add more shares to your holding without having to pay dealing costs or stamp duty.

Here are some points to watch out for. Some rights issues flop because the big financial institutions do not want them. If the price of the new shares is very near or above the price quoted on the stock market, something is wrong and normally you should not buy them. If you do not want the new shares, you may be able to sell your right to take up the rights issue in the stock market (termed 'nil paid rights') for a handy profit. Ask your stockbroker for more details and check if it will be worthwhile once you have paid his commission. If you do nothing the company will eventually sell your 'nil paid rights' for you and send you a cheque if there is a profit in it.

Scrip issues

Scrip, or capitalization, issues are different from rights issues in that the new shares that you receive are free, which is why they are sometimes known as bonus issues. However, as with rights issues, you get extra shares in proportion to the amount you already own – one for three, for example. The company merely increases its nominal capital and the market price of the shares usually adjusts to take account of the increased number of shares. Companies normally have scrip issues when they feel their share prices are getting too heavy i.e. expensive.

Individual investors seem to like having scrip issues and they can sometimes perk up the market price a bit, but remember to mark the changed prices carefully in your records. A forgotten scrip issue can seriously muddle your calculations.

14

Your Share Portfolio

There are theories galore about picking shares and every expert has a system. It might be based on looking at company data, analysing trends, or sticking a pin in the prices pages of the *Financial Times*. ProShare's system for analysing individual shares is set out in Chapter 6, but a successful share portfolio is not just about picking individual winners. It's about organizing all your investments to help you achieve your personal financial objectives.

• What kind of return do you want?

• How much risk can your nerves stand?

• Do you need income now?

• Or are you investing for a nest egg in the future?

Everyone has different requirements. But there are several broad categories that cover most stock market investors. The way you handle your portfolio depends on how you see yourself.

- *You earn a comfortable income with a pension but you want to build up some capital. You don't have a lot of time to devote to the stock market and you don't like taking big risks.*

You need a share portfolio to give you long-term capital appreciation and reasonable security. A mixture of blue chips and growth shares would be appropriate plus some unit and/or investment trusts.

Your share portfolio will not be particularly active and you will probably not trade shares regularly, but you need to make sure that you are beating inflation and at least doing as well, if not better, than the stock market as a whole. The FTSE APCIMs portfolio measures given in the weekend *Financial Times* will provide you with a benchmark against which you can measure the performance of your portfolio.

- *You are nearing or in retirement and you want to secure high-income return from your investments.*

You need to put a proportion of your capital in gilts and other fixed-interest investments when interest rates are high and timing this well is very important. Your share portfolio should include higher-yielding shares and blue chip companies. Even if income is your chief objective, your equity portfolio will be the main way to protect your capital from inflation and to supplement your income by taking some profits when interest rates are low.

- *You really enjoy playing the stock market and are prepared to spend time studying it. Even if you want to get a significant income out of your portfolio you may well choose to do it by investing for capital growth and taking profits on a regular basis.*

Your share portfolio should reflect your active interest. With a sound base of blue chip companies, you might opt for a selection of growth stocks plus special riskier situations – small cap shares, prospective bid candidates, recovery stocks and so on. But be sure that you have the time and interest to keep a careful eye on them day to day and only speculate with money you can afford to lose.

Whatever kind of investor you feel you are, there are some general rules of portfolio management that apply to all.

Spread the risks

You need to have enough different shares to give yourself a reasonable spread of investments. Even if you are going entirely for blue chips you must spread the risk – even the most solid companies can hit a bad patch. Aim to hold at least a handful of different shares. You should invest in several sectors rather than concentrating on just one. This doesn't mean that you shouldn't have more invested in, say, retailing if you think there is a recovery in consumer spending on the horizon; just do not put all your eggs in the same basket.

On the other hand, don't have too many shares. It will be a headache keeping track of them all. How many different shares you hold depends partly on the amount of money you have to invest. Dealing in very small quantities can be expensive because of minimum commission rates. Half a dozen to a dozen shares is a rough guideline for most private investors. Ideally, aim to invest at least £2,000 or certainly not less than £1,000 in each company in your portfolio. Invest less and commission charges will be proportionately high so your investments will have to work very hard to make a profit.

Check your portfolio

Get in the habit of checking the progress of your investments on a regular basis – noting daily, weekly or monthly movements in prices. It will give you some feel for the way certain shares or sectors react to general movements or events. It will show you which shares are earning their keep and which are lagging behind. Shares that move against the trend – fall when the market rises, or rise when it falls – are giving you a buy or sell sign well worth heeding. However, you should not pay too much attention to daily stock market fluctuations. You should invest with a long-term view and five years is a sensible minimum period of investment to have in mind.

When to sell

Selling shares well is almost more important than choosing which ones to buy. Never mind paper profits. The only profits which matter are the ones you take, the money you put in the bank.

The basic rule is to let profits run, and to cut losses quickly. Often, it seems, private investors do exactly the opposite. It is easy to persuade yourself that duds need more time, and will come right and if you take that profit winner, you can afford to hang on to the loser a little longer. Do not do it. In practice, someone in the market always knows more than you. Listen to what the share price is telling you. A little dip may not matter, but a consistent fall tells you that other people are selling. They probably have a good reason for it. Try to find out what the reason is by looking in the financial press or asking your broker, and if you feel it is appropriate, sell your shares.

It is important not to panic and sell whenever a share price falls. Only the most active investors with the time and expertise to follow the stock market should be constantly buying and selling on a regular basis. If you hold a well-researched, solid and balanced portfolio of investments, a fall in the value of one of your shares should be offset by your other investments and it should be possible to hold for the longer term.

Stop-loss system

Some people, particularly more active investors, swear by a stop-loss system. When you buy a share, you make a mental note to sell should the price fall by more than, say 20 per cent of the purchase price. Assume that you have bought shares for 100 pence (£1). If the share price fell below 80p, you would automatically sell your shares. Stop-loss limits should not be adjusted as share prices fall or they will be ineffective. It takes discipline to do it, and sometimes losers bounce back, and you end up selling a good share. But, in general, a stop-loss system is sensible. It means you never lose more than about 20 per cent, plus dealings costs, on any one share.

Running your profits

If you pick a winner, stay with it while it keeps going up. Others are buying it because they think it is good and perhaps they know more than you. Once shares start moving, they tend to develop a momentum. Success generates success. Fast risers attract attention, and more buyers come in.

You can use a stop-loss system with winners too. Trail the stop-loss level up behind the share price as it rises. If it slips more than, say, 20 per cent from the peak, take the profits. In other words if the share price moves up from a purchase price of 100p to 200p, you would sell if the share price fell to 160p (200p less 20 per cent). This is known as a rolling stop-loss. You never get out at the top that way – only luck can ensure you do that – but you never let big profits slip completely away.

Others advocate selling half of your holding in any share when it doubles, so that the shares you keep have effectively cost you nothing. That works for some, but it takes skill and good fortune to buy a winner. It seems a shame to cut half of your possible gain as it might really be getting going.

It is important to have a system, and impose self-discipline when it comes to selling shares. Otherwise you will let your portfolio drift, and find yourself holding the duds and selling the good shares.

Timing

You should also try to remember there are times – sometimes years – when the going will not be so good. You do not have to be an economic genius to sense when things are getting tougher. The stock market is usually among the first indicators. When interest rates are rising and perhaps the pound is under pressure, you know life is going to become more difficult for companies and subsequently the stock market. A falling or 'bear' market can create panic amongst small investors who rush to sell their holdings before share prices fall further. However, this is often the worst thing to do and here are some points to remember:

- Historically, falls in share prices, even significant falls caused by stock market crashes, even out over time. For example, the FTSE All Share Index was back to the level it had reached before the crash of October 1987 within two years and had more than doubled its pre-crash value within ten years.*

- Good and well-researched investment decisions should withstand a bear market (a falling market) as well as a bull market (a rising market). Remember that share prices are falling due to a lack of confidence in the market as a whole and not because of inherent problems with the company in which you are invested.

- Losses incurred on paper do not become real until you sell your shares, therefore it is best not to sell shares when markets are low unless you have to for a specific purpose. If you hang on, past experience shows that the market is likely to recover and you will be able to sell your shares at a better price in the future.

Many of the points that have been made previously about reducing the risk of stock market investment apply particularly in a falling market, where it is very important to have a

*Source: CSO FINSTATS.

long-term perspective and a balanced portfolio. You might like to adopt a drip-feed approach to investment, known as 'pound cost averaging', putting a little money in the stock market at regular intervals. This means that you will be buying shares at different times and at different prices, sometimes high and sometimes low, but overall you will pay a price somewhere in the middle, and avoid investing a lump sum at the top of the market. Investing in unit and investment trust saving schemes and participating in an investment club are easy ways to adopt this approach. Chapter 17 is dedicated to investment clubs and their benefits. Many more experienced investors view a falling market as an opportunity to purchase what are fundamentally good investments at a bargain price.

ProShare supplies a free Investor Update 10 entitled 'What to do when the market falls'.*

---

*See **Chapter 16**, pp. 138–40, for a complete list of Investor Updates and details of how to obtain them.

15

Investor Protection

The single most important phrase for any investor to understand is '*Caveat Emptor*' – 'Buyer Beware'. No one cares, or can care, quite as much about what happens to your hard-won cash as you do. This is not a cynical point of view. It is a statement of fact. In many ways, it is a reason for writing this book – a simple practical guide to the investment world that, hopefully, explains the basics. Knowledge and understanding is, and should be, everyone's best protection against being misled, cheated or simply being given bad advice.

When it comes to money, ignorance is certainly not bliss. It is irresponsibility. This is not to say that sensible people do not fall victim to bad advice. The mis-selling of personal pensions referred to in Chapter 11 is an obvious example. When you hand over your money, or take advice, you must be as certain as you can be about the credentials and competence of the people or institutions who are giving it.

There is a mass of legislation designed to prevent fraud and ensure certain standards of professional behaviour by those who handle money on behalf of the investing public. It is important to know your rights – and how to complain when things go wrong. But equally you should bear in mind that no system can, or ever will, completely eradicate the possibility of abuse. Your best safeguard is your own common sense, bolstered by real interest in what is happening to your money. You owe it to yourself to think clearly, ask questions and be a little sceptical. That way you will avoid being disappointed – or diddled.

Here are some basic dos and don'ts:

- Don't make investments as a result of a 'cold call'. If a salesperson phones you up or arrives at your front door without an appointment just accept the literature and say you'll get back to them if you are interested. If you have signed on the dotted line you are entitled to a 14-day 'cooling off' period during which you may change your mind and get your money back.

- Don't invest in anything that promises unusually high returns for low or no risk. There is almost always a catch. If it looks too good to be true it probably is.

- Don't invest in anything you don't understand. Many people fail to ask basic questions because they think it makes them look ignorant. That gives unscrupulous salespeople the chance to baffle them.

- Don't deal with firms or individuals who contact you from overseas. This includes signing up with Internet brokers based overseas. They may entice you with cheap dealing costs, but you will not be covered by UK legislation and regulations if things go wrong.

- Do check the credentials of everyone you deal with even if they have been recommended by friends or family.

- Do always read the small print.

- Do make sure cheques and deposits are made out to the institution whose investment products you are buying rather than to the intermediary, unless he can show he is authorized to accept your cash.

- Do keep all records of transactions and agreements carefully, to avoid misunderstanding and help if you have to make a complaint.

- Do make sure you know whether the person giving you financial advice is genuinely independent – or whether they are 'tied' to one particular company. You have a legal right to know.

These common-sense suggestions should help you avoid most potential pitfalls. There is a regulatory body designed to protect investors. The Financial Services Authority (FSA) is an independent, non-government body, and is the main watchdog overseeing the regulation of the financial services industry in the UK. The FSA authorizes firms or individuals to carry on business, imposes standards for professional behaviour and competence, makes regular checks on their members and will intervene if there is a dispute between a member firm and a customer.

To find out more about the regulator and its role, visit the FSA website at www.fsa.gov.uk

Investors' compensation scheme

However careful you are, things can go wrong. Investment firms can go bust, mishandle clients' money or give negligent advice that results in loss. If any of these things happen, you may have a claim for compensation under the Financial

Services Act, provided the firm you dealt with was authorized. Individuals can claim for a maximum amount of £50,000. If your claim is successful you will receive a maximum of £48,000 – the first £30,000 in full plus 90 per cent of the next £20,000. It is important to understand the limitations of the compensation scheme – and the fact that it does not cover investment losses due to a fall in the stock market.

When you choose a stockbroker, one of the things you might ask is if the firm has its own insurance to protect clients over and above the level provided by the ICS. If you have a complaint that you can't resolve with your stockbroker there is a complaints and arbitration procedure, the details of which are detailed on the FSA website.

The FSA produces a number of free brochures explaining the system of investor protection and helpful advice on what you should look out for. You can obtain these from the website or by telephoning the FSA Leaflet line.*

*See **Chapter 16, Useful Addresses,** pp. 141–2, for these contact telephone numbers.

16

ProShare

Since the early 1980s millions of people have been introduced to the stock market in a variety of ways, and the number of shareholders has increased from around 3 million in 1979 to around 12 million today. Millions of people became shareholders for the first time as their building societies turned themselves into banks and floated on the stock market. Throughout the 1980s and early 1990s people who had never owned shares before found it was easy, inexpensive and profitable to invest as the huge formerly state-owned utilities like British Telecom and the gas and electricity industries were transformed into major commercial organizations. In addition, many people have become investors for the first time through employee share schemes, which were introduced in 1979. But this is just the first step. To many the stock market still seems like a baffling and rather frightening place. Where do you go for advice and help? What does all the jargon mean? How can the ordinary investor ever keep up with the professionals? The mystique surrounding the stock market is one of the main reasons why relatively few of those who have bought privatization shares have gone on to invest in others.

ProShare was founded in 1992 as an independent, not-for-profit organization that provides independent information and a variety of services designed to help and encourage private investors. One of the main challenges for ProShare has been to ensure that potential and existing shareholders have access to unbiased information and advice about the stock market. ProShare does that through an extensive education programme and the production of user-friendly guidance on investment. It also provides information and assistance to investment clubs, which are an ideal way to learn about investing. ProShare lobbies Government and the relevant industry bodies to ensure that individual investment operates in a suitable tax and regulatory framework.

This book, for instance, aims to help the new stock market investor take their first steps in stock market investment, complemented by a comprehensive range of other useful products. ProShare's products and services available at the time of writing are as follows:

The Investor's Toolkit (£39.50 inc. p&p) £33.50 discounted price for *Investor's Handbook* readers

This paper-based system enables private investors and investment clubs to assess accurately the past performance of a company, whether the people who run the company are doing a good job, and to decide whether the share is good value for money at the price it is today. All this information is completed on a four-page Share Appraisal Form, which the user fills out him or herself. There is a plain English manual to explain each one of the seven sections. It is so easy to understand that in no time at all even the most inexperienced investor will understand how it works.

Introduction to Annual Reports and Accounts (£4.95 inc. p&p)

A simple guide to the main features in a company's annual report and accounts, including details on what to look for and how to interpret the information.

The Investor's Guide to Information Sources (£5.95 inc. p&p)

This guide takes the effort out of tracking down the most useful sources of information from daily newspapers to reference publications and investment analysis sites. It includes a summary of contents, a rating and a ProShare comment on each information source and a new expanded Internet section.

Portfolio Management System (£4.95 inc. p&p)

This simple but effective paper-based system will enable you to keep track of your portfolio and account to the Inland Revenue. The guide has been updated to include the latest budget changes.

To obtain any of the products mentioned, please write unless otherwise stated, enclosing a cheque made payable to ProShare (UK) Limited for the correct amount to:

ProShare (UK) Limited
Centurion House
24 Monument Street
London
EC3R 8AQ

Or call on 020 7394 5200 to order any of the products by credit card. Further information and a secure ordering facility is available at the ProShare website at www.proshare.org.

ProShare Investor Updates

Also available are ProShare's Investor Updates, a series of free factsheets for individual investors, which support ProShare's mission to make investing in shares more accessible to more people. Some of the factsheets cover basic subjects such as the advantages of stock market investment and the things to think about before you invest. Others, pointing out useful sources of stock market information and the different taxes that may be incurred when buying and selling shares, are relevant for new and experienced investors alike. The full range of titles, with a brief description, is as follows:

1. **'Investing in the stock market'** – covering the potential benefits to be gained from investing in the stock market and the things to consider before you start, this Update is ideal for anyone considering investment for the first time.

2. **'Choosing the right investment for you'** – this covers the relationship between risk and reward, the different circumstances that will affect your choice of investment and offers some golden rules for beginners.

3. **'Where to go to get investment advice'** – this Update gives information on who to go to for advice on investing in company shares, investment trusts, unit trusts and ISAs.

4. **'How to invest'** – this Update explains the mechanics of investing and covers the different types of services available when investing in shares, collective investments, gilts and ISAs.

5. **'Where to get investment information'** – useful for new and experienced investors alike, this Update provides invaluable information on many sources of stock market information available from newspapers to on-line services.

6. **'Shareholders' rights'** – a simple guide to your entitlements as a shareholder in a company, covering voting, company literature and dividend payments.

7. **'Taxes on share ownership'** – this Update gives details of the taxes you have to pay when buying and selling shares, and on the income from them, including indexation figures and the tapering system for CGT.

8. **'What is a nominee?'** – this explains the implications of holding your shares in a nominee account, the questions you should ask your broker when considering a nominee and the protection of assets. ProShare's Nominee Code is also explained.

9. **'How should I hold my shares?'** – this update explains the implications of CREST, the electronic system for transferring UK shares from seller to buyer. It explains the options available to individual investors under CREST.

10. **'What to do when the market falls'** – this update suggests some practical tactics to use in a falling market and some opportunities. It also explains stop-loss systems.

11. **'ISA: The Individual Savings Account'** – this update gives details of the Individual Savings Account and explains the various options available to savers and investors.

12. 'On-line services for the private investor' – an intro-duction to the services available on the Internet for private investors. Including company websites, portfolio management systems and on-line trading.

13. 'Investing for Children' – an update that explores the dif-ferent options available for anyone interested in saving for children.

14. 'Investing in Smaller Quoted Companies' – this update suggests some practical guidelines when considering investing in Smaller Quoted Companies.

15. 'Employee Share Plans' – an introduction to employee share plans, including the new, all-employee share plan.

16. 'Investing in Overseas Markets' – this update looks at how best to invest overseas, and highlights issues which the private investor should be aware of.

17. 'Investing in New Issues' – this update outlines the main points you should address when considering investing in new issues.

All of the Updates mentioned here can be read or down-loaded from the ProShare website at www.proshare.org. If you do not have Internet access they can be obtained by send-ing a stamped, self-addressed A4 envelope, with 39p postage attached, to ProShare Investor Updates, Centurion House, 24 Monument Street, London EC3R 8AQ. Please indicate clearly which Updates are required.

The ProShare website contains over 700 pages of up-to-date, easy-to-understand information which can be down-loaded free-of-charge. The site is completely independent and free of advertising. It contains a wide range of information including a facility to manage portfolios on-line, up-to-date daily news stories on the hot topics in the world of investment and personal finance, and a report and accounts service, which will allow users to order a company's most up-to-date report and accounts. Other features include on-line private investor training, real-time share prices and a comprehensive guide to information sources for private investors.

Useful Addresses

The Association of Private Client Investment Managers and Stockbrokers
112 Middlesex Street
LONDON E1 7HY
– publish a free directory of private client stockbrokers

The Association of Investment Trust Companies
Tel: 020 7282 5555
Web: www.itsonline.co.uk
– contact for helpful leaflets for investors

The Association of Unit Trusts and Investment Funds
Tel: 020 7831 08980
Web: www.investmentfunds.co.uk
– contact for helpful leaflets for investors

British Government Stocks –
To obtain a free booklet 'Investing in Gilts – the Private Investor's Guide to Investing in British Government Stocks' –
Tel: 01452 398080

Financial Services Authority (FSA)
Contact to check basic information on firms and individuals, free of charge, and also to enquire about other financial services issues.
Web: www.fsa.gov.uk (central register, and to access other services)
Consumer Helpline: 0845 606 1234
FSA Leaflet Line: 0800 917 3311

ProShare
– see Chapter 16, above, for all ProShare addresses/website/contact numbers.

17

Investment Clubs

Investing in the stock market is not just a way of building up capital or saving for your old age. As any keen investor will tell you, following the stock market is a fascinating business. Picking your shares, watching what happens to them, weighing up the economic news, learning to sniff out opportunities, looking out for problems, all these elements mean investors find the stock market a stimulating hobby. It can be made even more exciting when they can share their knowledge with others through an investment club.

Investment clubs have become a real phenomenon in the UK in recent years. They originated in the US over a hundred years ago, but have taken off in the UK where the number has grown from 350 to almost 10,000 in four years. Investors have found that clubbing together to invest in the stock market is profitable and fun.

ProShare believes that investment clubs are one of the most important ways of encouraging individuals to invest in the stock market and actively promotes their formation. ProShare has produced *The ProShare Investment Club Manual*, a definitive guide to setting up and running an investment club. If you are the sort of person who enjoys swapping ideas and knowledge you should consider starting one of your own with like-minded friends.

There are a host of advantages in pooling your stock market investments in this way. It can be expensive running your own portfolio, particularly if you only have a modest sum to invest. As we have seen, successful investment involves spreading the risk through buying a number of different shares in a variety of sectors. You may be able to achieve this more quickly, and at a lower cost, by pooling your resources through an investment club. It's like having your own unit trust without the management charges.

Doing your research is a crucial part of successful stock market investment, but it is time consuming. Club members can agree to look at different companies and sectors, maybe specializing in industries where they have particular knowledge or contacts. An investment club is the ideal forum for debating investment ideas. Everyone has their own point of view and discussion is a good way to ensure that sensible decisions are made after they have been properly considered. Many clubs invite guest speakers to talk about aspects of investment. If you're an absolute beginner you will learn from other members. If you are an experienced stock market investor it is an opportunity to get together with others who share the same interests.

Members agree how much money each should put in the 'pot' – £25 per member per month is the average subscription. Joining an investment club means that you are setting aside a regular sum for your stock market investment, which is a good savings discipline. It is important that everyone is comfortable with the amounts chosen and the subscription can be varied between members. You will probably be wise to wait until you have built up a reasonable sum – say £500 minimum before you make your first investment. Some clubs run fantasy portfolios to provide an element of fun to their club. If you do this for the first couple of months, you will have plenty of ideas for your first investment by the time your funds are sufficient.

The most successful investment clubs operate on the basis of co-operation between friends who enjoy meeting each other. You can have your monthly meetings anywhere from members' houses to the pub. Many clubs are made up of work colleagues, but it should be a sociable event so few clubs actually meet at a work place.

The laws relating to partnerships mean you can't have more than twenty members in an investment club. Between ten and fifteen is a sensible number to aim for. There will be enough of you to get the benefits of 'collective' investment but not to spoil the club atmosphere or make decision-making difficult. Don't rush to recruit that number at the start. It is important that the mix of members is right and that everyone agrees with the investment approach set out by the club at the outset. Similarly, don't worry if you don't think that you can recruit fifteen people by yourself. Get a couple of friends involved and ask them to mention to some of their friends and colleagues to see if they are interested. You will soon have enough for an initial 'exploratory' meeting.

How an investment club works

Of high importance is establishing how the members' investments will be accounted for so that everyone will know how well they are doing. There are different ways of running the fund. ProShare favours the unit valuation system, which is one of the simplest methods of monitoring the value of members' investments.

At the beginning, each £1 contributed gives members one unit. To work out the value of the units once the club starts investing, you simply divide the club's assets by the number of units. The fund is re-valued each month to create a new unit value, which is used to work out the number of units to be purchased with each month's cash subscriptions. Within this framework it is possible for new members to join and for others to buy extra units or sell part of their holding if necessary.

It is important that a club starts out on the right footing and *The ProShare Investment Club Manual* contains a draft constitution and rules that enable the club to be constituted very easily according to the rules set out by stockbrokers and the financial regulators. You must then decide who is to chair meetings, who is to look after the administration, where the money will be held, who will have access to it, and what kind of stockbroking service you require. A number of brokers now provide dedicated comprehensive services for investment clubs, often at preferential rates, so it pays to shop around. The *ProShare Guide to Stockbroking Services for Investment Clubs* (free) will help.

The ProShare Investment Club Manual is the ultimate 'how to' guide to setting up and running an investment club, containing tax and accounting information. It is supported by lots of useful information and questions and answers to get you started. If you want to find out more before purchasing the *Manual*, the book *A Way to Learn; A Way to Earn* (priced £4.99) covers how easy and enjoyable it is to set up an investment club with your friends, work colleagues and family. It is backed up with many real-life examples of ordinary people who have made a success of investing in the stock market with others.

The ProShare Investment Club Manual usually costs £29.50, but is available to readers of *The Investor's Handbook* for £25. At the time of writing, the price of the manual also includes a first year's free membership to ProShare Investment Clubs, which entitles the club to a regular magazine *Dividend* for each of its club members, a free sample copy of *Company REFS*, access to the PIC Help-line and entry into various competitions. There is also a dedicated, password-protected investment-club website for members at www.proshareclubs.co.uk.

Please telephone 020 7394 5200 to order a copy of the manual by credit card or write to ProShare at the address given on p. 137 enclosing a cheque made payable to ProShare (UK) Limited for £25.

You can also obtain more information, or order *The Manual* and *A Way to Learn; A Way to Earn* from the ProShare website at www.proshare.org.

A to Z of Investment

A **Aggregate Demand** The total demand in the economy for all goods and services.

AIM Alternative Investment Market.

Assets are what a company owns – land, machinery, stocks, cash and investments. Deduct liabilities like loans and creditors and you get NET ASSET VALUE – what the company might be worth if it were wound up.

At Best is an instruction to your stockbroker to buy or sell shares for the best price available.

Audit A professional, independent examination of the accounts of a company.

B **Balance Sheet** A statement of the assets and liabilities of a company at the end of the financial year.

Bear Market A market that is moving downwards.

Bed and Breakfast Selling shares and then buying them back again the next day to mitigate Capital Gains Tax.

Bid Price The price at which you sell shares.

Big Bang The day of sweeping changes in the securities industry: October 27 1986.

Blue Chip A big, well-known company whose shares are considered low risk.

Bond A debt where the issuer pays a fixed rate of interest per year and the principal amount on a stated maturity date.

Bull Market A rising market.

C **Call Option** The right, but not the obligation, to buy stock or shares at an agreed price up to a date in the future.

Capital An investor's savings and wealth, or a company's share capital and resources.

Capital Gains Tax A tax on the increase in value of assets sold in a particular year.

Commission The fee that a broker may charge clients for dealing on their behalf.

Convertible Loan Stocks pay fixed interest but can be converted into shares at a given price at set times.

CREST The UK settlement system for shares.

CUM Latin for 'with'. If a share is quoted CUM dividend or CUM rights issue it means that it still bears the entitlement and this is reflected in the price.

D **Depreciation** is the financial equivalent of wear and tear. Businesses deduct a certain amount from profits to reflect the decline in value of plant and machinery.

Deregulation Attempting to make a market more efficient by removing or reducing restrictions.

Discretionary Account Your stockbroker or financial adviser can make investment decisions without necessarily consulting you.

Dividend The part of profit (after tax) set aside to pay shareholders.

Dividend Yield The return from the income, expressed as a percentage of the money paid for a share.

E **Earnings Per Share** The amount of profit that can be assigned to each share.

Equities is another term for ordinary shares – the risk-sharing part of a company.

EX A share price may be quoted as EX dividend or EX rights. It means the buyer will not have entitlement to the recent dividend payment or rights issue.

F **Flat Yield** The income return on a fixed-interest investment at current price.

Flotation When a company's shares are brought to the stock market and quoted for the first time.

FTSE 100 Index The *Financial Times* Stock Exchange Index 100; offers up-to-the-minute indications of market performance; sometimes called 'The Footsie'.

G **Gearing** Company borrowing as a proportion of share-holders' funds. A highly geared company is a riskier investment but when times are good earnings grow faster.

Gilts/Gilt Edged Securities issued by the government. Sometimes known as government bonds.

Goodwill Intangible assets, such as reputation.

Gross describes the value before deductions. An investment may be described as yielding 10 per cent gross – that means before deduction of income tax.

H **Hedge** An investment that gives protection – against inflation, for instance, or currency risks.

I **Index-linked** means the value or return from an investment is tied to the rate of price inflation.

Inflation A persistent and appreciable increase in the general level of prices; also a fall in the value of money.

Insider Dealing If directors, stockbrokers, or others close to the company or members of the public deal shares on the basis of confidential information they are guilty of a criminal offence.

ISA Individual Savings Account.

Issue Price Price at which shares are first offered to investors when a company floats on the stock market.

Interim Dividend A dividend declared part way through a company's financial year, authorized solely by the directors.

Investment Trust A company investing in the equity of other companies; investment trust shares are quoted on the Stock Exchange.

L **Liabilities** Financial obligations of a company.

Liquidity How easily a company or individual can turn assets into cash (without loss of value).

Liquidity ratio The value of liquid assets compared with current liabilities.

Listing The process of having shares quoted in the London Stock Exchange.

Longs Market term for government stocks (gilts) that have over fifteen years to go until they are due to be repaid.

M **Market Maker** A stock market trader who offers to buy and sell shares and bonds at all times.

Mediums Market term for gilts (government securities) that have between five and fifteen years to go before repayment.

Middle Market Price Halfway between the buying and selling prices of a share. Most newspapers use the middle market price in their daily stock market lists for convenience.

N **Net** means after deductions. A net return on an investment describes its value after tax has been deducted.

Net Asset Value The net assets of a company divided by the number of shares it has issued.

New Issue A company coming to the market for the first time or issuing extra shares.

Nominal Value means the face or par value of shares or other investments as opposed to the market value – what you can buy or sell at now.

Nominee The legal agreement where one person or firm holds shares on behalf of another.

O **Offer for Sale** A method of bringing a company to the market. The public can apply for shares directly at a fixed price. A prospectus containing details of the sale must be printed in a national newspaper.

OEICs Open Ended Investment Companies.

Offer Price Price at which you buy a share.

Ordinary Shares Shares where the dividend varies with company profits.

Oversubscribed is when a new issue attracts more applications than there are shares available.

P **Par** Nominal price of a share or bond as stated on its certificate; it may have no relation to the market value.

Penny Shares The shares in companies that are at a very low price.

Portfolio A collection of securities owned by an investor.

Preference Shares rank before ordinary shares for dividend payments, and in the event of a company being wound up preference shares must be repaid before equity holders get anything. Preference shares offer a fixed return – the dividends on ordinary shares go up and down depending on profits.

Price/Earnings Ratio The ratio between share price and earnings; sometimes called the 'p/e ratio'.

Premium Upward difference between issue price of a share or other investment and its market value.

Profit and Loss Account Accounts detailing revenue and costs, profits (or losses) of a company.

Prospectus A necessary legal requirement for any company issuing shares to the public, containing relevant information about the company and the planned share issue.

Q **Quote** The current price for buying and selling a share offered by a market maker.

R **Rights Issue** An invitation to existing shareholders to purchase additional shares in the company.

Rolling Settlement means that shares have to be paid for within a specific number of days following each transaction.

S **SEAQ** The Stock Exchange Automated Quotations System; a database of share prices, which is continually updated.

Secondary Market Market place for trading in securities that are not new issues.

SETS The Stock Exchange Electronic Trading Service. The new 'order driven' system used for trading in shares in larger companies.

Settlement is when Stock Exchange transactions are paid for.

Shorts Market term for gilts (government securities) that have less than five years to go before repayment.

Spread The difference between the market-maker's bid and offer prices for a share.

Stag One who buys securities new on the market (new issues) in the hope of selling them quickly for a higher price.

Stock Any fixed interest security.

Stockbroker Someone who buys and sells shares and other Stock Exchange securities on behalf of clients.

Suspension Trading in a share can be halted by the Stock Exchange – a company might ask for a temporary suspension of dealings – if a take-over bid is under discussion for instance. Sometimes a suspension means bad news is on the way.

T **Tender** A way of auctioning shares or gilt-edged securities to the highest bidders. A guide is announced – then investors have to make up their own minds how much to offer for the number of shares they want.

Touch Competing market makers quote slightly different prices for a share. The touch is the difference between the best bid price and the lowest offer price.

Tranche When some part of an issue comes to the market at a different time and possibly at a different price.

Turnover Volume of business over a period of time.

U **Underwrite** To agree to buy securities that may be left unsold after a new issue, a fee will be charged; also to provide funds in matters of insurance.

Undated Securities have no repayment date.

Unit Trusts UK savings schemes run by specialists that invest in securities.

W **Warrants** A certificate that gives the holder the right to buy shares at a given price and date.

Working Capital is the cash needed to finance the everyday running of a business such as the payment of salaries and the purchase of raw materials. Most companies that go bust do so because a shortage of working capital leads to a cash flow crisis.

Y **Yield** is the annual rate you get on an investment through payment of dividends or interest.

Z **Zero-Coupon Bonds** do not pay interest. They are issued at a deep discount to the redemption price so that the investor receives the return in the form of capital gain rather than income.

Index

Index

Index

Index